BREAKING YOUR R_X ADDICTION HABIT

With Amino Acids and Nutrient Therapy

Billie Jay Sahley, Ph.D., and
Katherine M. Birkner, C.R.N.A., Ph.D.

Pain & Stress Publications
San Antonio, Texas
1996

Copyright © 1996 by Pain & Stress Publications

Note to Readers

This material is not intended to replace services of a physician, nor is it meant to encourage diagnosis and treatment of illness, disease, or other medical problems by the layman. This book should not be regarded as a substitute for professional medical treatment and while every care is taken to ensure the accuracy of the content, the authors and the publisher cannot accept legal responsibility for any problem arising out of experimentation with the methods described. Any application of the recommendations set forth in the following pages is at the reader's discretion and sole risk. If you are under a physician's care for any condition, he or she can advise you as to whether the programs described in this book are suitable for you.

No part of this publication may be reproduced, stored in a retrieval system, or transmitted in any form or by any means, electronic, mechanical, photocopying, recording, or otherwise, without the prior written permission of the authors.

This publication has been compiled through research resources at The Pain & Stress Center, San Antonio, Texas 78229.

Second Edition
Printed in the U.S.A.

Additional copies amy be ordered from:
The Pain & Stress Center
5282 Medical Drive, Suite 160, San Antonio, Texas 78229-6023

Library of Congress Catalog Card Number: 96-71285

ISBN: 1-889391-04-2

Dedicated ...

To a new generation of physicians, therapists, and educators who seek to find the natural alternative that frees the addicted from the prison of prescription and street drugs and gives them God's greatest gift—the freedom to make a choice.

To my beloved mother, who started me on the path of understanding the power of the mind and using it.

And to the Lord, for always lighting my path.

B.J.S.

There is no such thing as an impossible dream.
If you believe it, you can make it happen.

Acknowledgments

Our sincere appreciation and thanks to:

The staff of the Pain & Stress Center of San Antonio, Texas (past and present) for their support and dedication to helping people with addiction problems.

The many physicians across the country using orthomolecular medicine who share their research and give us constant encouragement.

Our patients, who teach us something everyday.

Table of Contents

What Is Addiction?   7

Withdrawal And Recovery   15
    Recovery Time–Freedom From Pills–Benzodiazepine Withdrawal Table–Xanax Taper Table–Phenobarbital Withdrawal Table–Reduction Procedures–Wiithdrawal Symptoms by Addictive Substances–Anxiety–Grief Reactions– Stress Reactions–Medication Withdrawal Procedure

Alcoholism And Its Treatment   26
    Progression of Drinking Symptoms–Symptoms Of Alcohol Withdrawal (Mild or Early)–Symptoms Of Alcohol Withdrawal (Late or Severe)–Factors Leading To Malnutrition In Alcoholism–Alcohol/Drug-Induced Nutritional Deficiencies–Treatment–Metabolism Of Alcohol–Nutrient And Amino Acid Program For The Therapeutic Treatment Of Alcoholism

Nicotine And Caffeine Addiction And Treatment   35
    Nicotine Withdrawal Program–Caffeine–Caffeine Content Of Various Substances–Caffeine Detox Procedure

Amino Acids For Therapy   40
    GABA–L-Glutamine, The Surprising Brain Fuel– Phenylelanine–DLPA And Depression–Treatment–Key Factors Of DLPA–L-Tyrosine–Tyrosine Or DLPA Cannot Be Taken With The Following Medications–L-Tryptophan– L-Cysteine–L-Carnitine–Dietary Sources Of L-Carnitine– Heart Disease–Cirrhosis And Carnitine–Taurine–Amino Acids And Their Effect On The Body–Drug-Nutrient Interactions–Amino Acids And Clinical Conditions And Diseases

Supplement   64
    Esterfied C–Melatonin–Vitamins And Nutrients That Aid In Recovery From Drugs–Amino Acids And Nutrients That Can Be Used For Recovery From Substance Abuse Dependency On A Daily Basis–Trends In Substance Abuse– Paxil–Effexor–Zoloft–Serzone–Risperdal–Prozac–Luvox– Anabuse

References   76

Introduction

Orthomolecular therapy means supplying the cells with the right mixture of nutrients. Many diseases are known to be the result of the wrong balance of essential nutrients in the body. Adjusting the diet, eliminating junk foods and ingesting the proper doses of essential vitamins, minerals and amino acids, can correct the chemical imbalance of disease.

The orthomolecular approach helps patients become more aware of our dangerously polluted environment and nutrient-stripped refined foods. The orthomolecular approach is both corrective and preventative. Meganutrient therapy has become a part of orthomolecular medicine. While it is becoming widely recognized that orthomolecular therapy cures patients by correcting brain chemical imbalances, it is little known that in certain combinations meganutrients can be as immediately effective as potent painkillers or tranquilizers. Meganutrients treat the whole person's biochemical imbalances; they can be of immediate and long term benefit. The type of treatment offered by orthomolecular doctors and therapists varies, but the mainstream of work focuses upon meganutrient therapy and diagnostic tests, and treatment with adequate nutrients is a distinguishing characteristic of orthomolecular medicine.

Orthomolecular therapy takes into consideration that every individual is biochemically unique. Every patient has a very different nutrient and amino acid requirement, and with application of this therapy, each individual's need is met, and the mind and body are in a state of homeostasis–a condition where everything in the body is in balance and capable of resisting environmental changes, while regulating internal metabolic function.

Every tissue of the body is affected by nutrition. Under conditions of poor nutrition, the kidneys stop filtering, the stomach stops digesting, the adrenals stop secreting and other organs follow suit.

Good nutrition is essential to the preservation of health and the prevention of disease. Meganutrient therapy has become a part of orthomolecular medicine. It has continually expanded and now recognizes that all of our biological interactions with food, water, air and light are an important part of good health and prevention of illness, if taken in proper amounts.

1

WHAT IS ADDICTION?

Millions have died and millions will die because of their addiction.

Addictions affect one out of three people. In the United States alone, more than fifteen million people are affected by the use of some type of toxic substance. It is well established that tranquilizers, antidepressants, pain medication, substance abuse, and alcohol constitute a major health problem in the U.S. Approximately 300,000 men, women, and children will die prematurely every year from a wide range of prescription drugs, alcohol, and substance related problems and illnesses including cancer, heart disease, suicide, and homicide, as well as highway fatalities and other accidents. Addictions can and do affect people from all social classes, of all degrees of intelligence, and all professional levels.

According to the President's Commission on Mental Health, a fourth of the citizens in the U.S. suffer from some type of severe emotional stress. Another study shows that 80 percent of all Americans feel the need to reduce stress in their daily lives. *Harrison's Principles of Internal Medicine* states 50 to 80% of all disease is stress induced. All stress-related conditions are similar whether manifested as psychiatric or general medical problems. Does stress lead to addiction? YES!

A cry for help from the American public has gone out: How can they reduce the harmful impact of stress on their physical and mental well-being? Many have come to expect instant relief from emotions and negative feelings, and find it necessary to look for instant pleasure that is chemically induced. If you swallow one pill or a combination of prescription pills the relief you feel is only brief. When you take pills you suffer emotional disfigurement. Given this information, records show that drugs—and a greater inclination to try them, once or twice or perhaps sporadically—fit conveniently into our stress-filled society. These substances allow the manipulation of moods by simply providing a brief escape for the user.

All substances of abuse either elevate or decrease consciousness and intensifies depressed moods. Escape is the primary factor, and the drug of choice will be the one the user feels will give him instant relief. A person who is addicted will always have to satisfy his addiction before he can move on to do anything else. Everyone has problems and the antidepressants, tranquilizers, pain pills, drugs, and alcohol make one feel these problems are not pressing...that you can put your worries and your life on hold. But prescription drugs and alcohol make problems unmanageable, unresolvable, and unbearable. Prescription drug and street drug users are thirty times more likely to commit suicide than the norm.

What predisposes a person to choose a particular substance? It is their availability through prescriptions or contacts, and finding the funds to pay for it. This is especially evident among teens and those even younger. We live in an addictive society, a society that has all the characteristics and exhibits all the effects of the alcoholic or prescription addict.

As health care professionals who work with addiction know, the most caring thing we can do is not to embrace the denial, but confront the disease. *The primary cause of the addict's problem is not psychological illness, but physical addiction.* An addiction is any process over which we are powerless. Prescription drugs, street drugs, and alcohol take control of a person, causing him to do and think things that are inconsistent with his personal values. It leads him to become more compulsive and obsessive.

A particular symptom of an addiction is the sudden need for the addict to destroy himself and others. He often lies, denies, and covers-up. The addictive personality feels compelled to lie and is unwilling to give up anything. He is unaware of what is going on inside of him. He does not have to deal with his anger, pain, depression, confusion, or even joy and love; he does not have these feelings, or feels them only vaguely. The addicted person stops relying on his knowledge and sense and relies on confused perceptions. During this time there is a lack of internal awareness that deadens his internal processes, which in turn allows him to remain addicted. The addicted person loses contact with himself and with other people around him.

An addictive substance dulls and distorts sensory input and output. The user does not receive information clearly nor does he process it correctly. He is unable to assimilate feedback information or respond to it accurately. Since addicts are not in touch with themselves, they present a distorted self to the world. Addicts con people and eventually lose the ability to become intimate with others, even those they are closest to and love most—their family and their friends.

Addicts are aware that something is very wrong, but the addictive thinking tells them that it could not possibly be their fault. This kind of thinking also tells them that they cannot make things right— that someone else will have to do it for them. An addiction absolves the users from having to take responsibility for their lives, and permits the assumption that someone or something outside themselves will swoop down to make things better or help them deal with what they are going through. Since addicts tend to be dependent and feel increasingly powerless and bad about themselves, the notion that they can take responsibility for their lives is inconceivable to them.

The longer the addict waits to be rescued, the worse the addiction becomes. Regardless of what they are addicted to, it takes more and more to create the desired effect, and no amount is ever enough! This includes antidepressants, tranquilizers, pain killers and alcohol. Before being ready for recovery, the individual must often hit bottom. At this time a new sense of reality surfaces: they no longer want to hide their addiction, they want help.

Addictions can be divided into two major categories:
1) addiction to substances such as alcohol, prescription and street drugs, nicotine, caffeine.
2) addictions to processes such as gambling and shopping.

For the addict to come to terms with the possibility that he could be addicted to both, and therefore must recover from both, is staggering. According to Alcoholics Anonymous, the addicted person cannot remain static; he must either get better or worse. Both addiction and recovery are processes.

The addicted personality is one that has been enslaved—a prisoner of his own mind, condemned by his own guilt, fear, and fear of failure. This is one of the reasons he must hit bottom before he admits he is out of control and needs help with his fears—fear of living, fear of loss of control. The addict must not concern himself with how he got there, only with recovery, living one day at a time. He cannot allow fear of the future to set in, as this leads to almost certain failure. An addict grieves for the past and all of the time he wasted, the people he hurt, the lives he destroyed. But his fear of the future brings forth a new set of problems, anxieties, fears, and phobias. Now he must become responsible and face the realities he has avoided, denied, and pushed aside.

The most important and enduring part of the global response to the addiction problem has been intellectual. Substance abuse therapists and researchers around the world have sought to understand why people try to escape through the use of drugs and alcohol, as well as the long-term negative effects on the brain.

Researchers have found that there is a specific receptor in the brain for morphine. Shortly thereafter, it was discovered that there were natural brain chemicals that fit these receptors. This finding opened the door to a new understanding of the psychiatric profile of substance abusers and their brain function.

Researchers have determined there is a neurochemical imbalance that makes the alcoholic incapable of drinking normally. His body simply does not process alcohol correctly. And unlike other psychoactive drugs, alcohol does not target specific parts of nerve cells or neurons but seems to enter cell membranes and sabotage the nervous system indiscriminately.

The National Institute of Mental Health is studying how alcohol affects certain cells in the brain to induce a sedative effect. The complex workings of the brain provide a map with unique pathways for the addicted. Although some become sedated, others become agitated, angry, depressed, melancholy, anxious, excited and fearful. The brain chemistry holds the key. Deficiencies or imbalances are thought to be the result of genetic anomalies, metabolic disturbances due to stress, or the destructive effects of prescription drugs, alcohol, or drug abuse.

One theory on addiction, according to Janice Phelps, M.D., is that it is due to a biochemical defect with which certain individuals are born. The physiologic flaw begins at least in part in the adrenal glands. This defect consists of a sugar imbalance or dysmetabolism and a chronic biochemical depression or genetic depression. Genetic depression is a chronic physiological and biochemical depression that is passed from generation to generation in some families, though not necessarily affecting all family members. Genetic depression is very closely related to addictiveness, conceivably arising from the same physiological defect in the brain.

Genetic depression may arise in infancy or childhood, or it may not appear until the teen years or even adulthood. It may go unrecognized if it has been present so long that for that person it seems normal; the person living with it has become an expert at concealing it.

The signs of genetic depression are many and varied. Signs of this imbalance in infants are indigestion or stomachaches. In older children, it might be manifested as anxiety, learning disabilities, attention problems, or hyperactivity. In the adult, headaches, backaches, and stomachaches are common, as are anxiety and worry. Sleep disorders, appetite changes, lack of energy, and constant fatigue may also be present. Even changes in sexual response may be related to depression. A defect in the chemical communication from the brain to the adrenals seems to provide the single key.

The signs and symptoms of depression must be recognized, but anxiety and depression are so similar at times that even physicians cannot tell the difference. The relationship between the pituitary-adrenal axis and depression must be understood. Some of the major symptoms include physical pain and symptoms, perhaps even mental illness in the genetically depressed person. With the underlying addictiveness or family history of addiction, many symptoms may be attributed to depression. Many addicted people do not realize they are depressed and have been depressed all of their lives.

According to Dr. Phelps, a good working definition of addiction is as follows: "An addiction is the compulsive and out-of-control use of any chemical substance that can produce recognizable and identifiable unpleasant withdrawal symptoms when use of the substance is stopped. Such addiction is driven by an inborn physiological hunger in the addictive person, and is frequently intimately related to depression." All addicting substances, from sugar to nicotine to narcotics, seem to give short-term relief from depression in the beginning. Later, the same substance aggravates it. The authors believe the degree of "normalcy," "relaxation" or feeling of well-being a person experiences from an addicting substance probably is related to the individual's degree of depression. There is no doubt that a link exists between depression and addiction. It plays an important role in the overall pattern of addiction and addictive behavior.

No one ever fully recovers from anxiety, insomnia, or depression while on drugs, whether the drugs are in the form of alcohol, street dope, or pharmaceutical-grade drugs. Stop the drugs and the anxiety comes back.

Millions of dollars are spent publicizing and promoting pharmaceuticals rather than researching them. The promotions are to convince all of us that the prescription products are useful and beneficial so that physicians will prescribe them and the public will request them. The pharmaceutical industry thrives on illness, not on wellness; it has no significant financial motivation to strive for wellness in society. Sick days pay, not well days.

Most physicians are unappreciative of the extent nutritional supplements plays in wellness. Many psychiatrists live under the illusion that anything below the brain cannot contribute to an emotionally healthy person—and amino acids and nutrients do not count. Most doctors' education regarding nutrition is only superficial and generally is limited to one semester in medical school. The greatest part of their nutrition education deals with caloric requirements and the recommended daily allowances. The recommended daily allowances are simply the bare minimum nutritional requirements to prevent the onset of states of deficiency. Yet a whole new world of healing awaits them with nutritional medicine. The brain is the most underfed organ in the body. Drugs certainly do not nourish, so how is the brain fed?

The late Carl C. Pfeiffer, M.D., Ph.D., renowned for his work in the field of orthomolecular medicine, summed up the challenge in what he calls "Pfeiffer's Law", which states, "We have found that if a drug can be found to do the job of medical healing, a nutrient can be found to do the same job. When we understand how a drug works, we can imitate its action with one of the nutrients."

The pharmaceutical giants in the early sixties began marketing a new class of drugs called the benzodiazepines or "minor" tranquilizers/sedatives. This was done to meet the commercial demands for anxiety relief. The most popular trade names of this class are Xanax, Valium, Tranxene, Halcion, Librium, Ativan, Dalmane, Loxitane, and Librax.

Benzodiazepines are available as commercial products, but they do not cure anxiety, depression, stress, or insomnia. These drugs exist because of the tremendous profits they generate for the pharmaceutical companies that manufacture and promote them. These companies spend millions entertaining physicians to convince them to prescribe these products. The resulting profits are made possible by the inherent addictive potential of these drugs and the patent protection of the drug manufacturers who hold exclusive rights for seventeen years. Thus, when users become dependent on particular drugs, the pharmaceutical companies stand to make huge profits. *Consumer Reports*, January 1993, gives an in-depth research report on Xanax, Halcion, and Prozac conclusion: they do not work! *Consumer Reports* stated Xanax, Halcion and Prozac all have histories of extensive potential for hazardous side effects including death. Latest published reports show physicians in the U.S. write more than a million prescriptions for Prozac each month. Zoloft and Paxil are close behind. Prescribed addiction has taken over.

A condition which baffles many drug victims is characterized by free-floating anxiety and panic attacks. These attacks can come without warning and seemingly without reason. This sends the poor, anxiety-ridden and confused person to the nearest emergency room. After admission, every conceivable test is administered; the physicians determine the cause is actually a panic and/or an anxiety attack which can take on the symptoms of a heart attack. Thirty percent of admissions in the emergency rooms in the United States are actually panic/anxiety attacks disguised as heart attacks.

Prescription drug dependents become addicts in large measure because they are unaware of natural alternatives and orthomolecular therapy. They make choices based on the convention that has taught them to trust their doctor and his medicines. These victims go through a long period of addiction denial. But denial is self-defeating. Addicts, and often their families as well, deny the addiction. Many never do admit it and never look at the situation honestly; it is too frightening for them to do so. Honest, open communication of feelings in a non-judgmental way is vital to breaking an addiction.

There appears to be agreement about the presence of the three major elements in the drug abuse problem: the drugs, the people who use them, and the social forces shaping, and in turn being influenced by, both of these. A recently coined term that fits the study of all three of these elements is "social pharmacology"; it now awaits new definitions and delineations of its role in the psychotropic (i.e., acting on the mind) drug abuse field.

From the enormous number of studies that provide some answers to the question of how widespread is drug and alcohol use, several tentative conclusions may be drawn. Marijuana appears to attract the greatest experimentation and narcotics the least, with other drugs following in between. Males tend to experiment more than females; persons who are better educated and with higher incomes tend to "try out" drugs more frequently than persons who are less educated and have lower incomes. Dr. Kenneth Blum, a pharmacologist, has shown the comparison of drug abuse with recreational drugs; he reveals the lack of consistency in society's approach to both. A person may be a confirmed alcoholic and be regarded as "sick" in our society. But one who habitually uses marijuana and is dependent on it psychologically will be viewed as a criminal, not a sick person, even if the social liability of both individuals is much the same. The attitude of many people is that society does not need either one: we already have ten million alcoholics, so why create a comparable class of addicts?

This attitude characterizes the thinking of the American public. Even drugs prescribed by a physician may not be good for you, and serious side effects as well as long-term addiction can occur. Those with emotional problems and chronic pain are potential victims of this, "it's okay to take" attitude. The Council on Patient Information and Education states, "Up to half of all prescription drugs are taken incorrectly" because people do not understand how toxic chemicals effect their brain and the possibility of dependency. The abuse of prescription drugs is one of the most pervasive problems in the United

States today. People take more than they need because of fear. Fear of anxiety, fear of depression, fear of loneliness, or fear their pain will come back.

When physicians give patients prescriptions for abusable drugs such as antidepressants, tranquilizers or pain killers they do not spend the time counseling the patients about dependency.

Senior citizens are a major target, especially when they have no family or a reliable source of information. Anxiety, depression and pain are the three major reasons why they begin taking abusable drugs. Most often their first prescription is for a benzodiazepine the most commonly prescribed medication in the world. Xanax is at the top of the list. Anyone who takes Xanax for an extended period, only a few weeks, risks a possible dependency to Xanax. Xanax is more addictive than Valium.

Important Warning:

RX Drugs Are Drugs

There are no drugs in pharmacology which cure anxiety, panic, phobias, insomnia, depression, allergies, arthritis, asthma, cardiac, diabetes, hypertension, hyperactivity, or inflammatory conditions, chronic pain, or disease.

There are many drugs which treat the symptoms of these disorders. However, many prescription drugs have a significant potential for long-term adverse or permanent drug side-effects.

When the word "addict" is used, it does not mean just the addict on street drugs. What it does mean is people from all walks of life, all ages, whole families. Even children are not immune if their parents allow them to take prescribed drugs such as antidepressants, tranquilizers, or stimulants; this, in fact, sets up a pattern for a lifetime with a chemical straightjacket.

2

WITHDRAWAL AND RECOVERY

Many of the symptoms experienced by those who want to withdraw from an addiction are anxiety related simply because of increasing uncertainty about whether they will succeed. Withdrawal reactions will vary a great deal from person to person. Some people can reduce the quantity and even drop tranquilizers without any problems, others have minor problems, and some have major withdrawal problems. **Caution must be taken by those who want to withdraw. You should not begin withdrawal unless you follow a program that advises you on how and what to do and what to expect.**

Withdrawal and recovery take time. Addiction does not happen overnight and your system cannot release all the accumulated toxins at once. There are only a few drugs that give the proper therapeutic action. People who regularly take tranquilizers, antidepressants, and pain medication can often experience the following side effects: depression, anxiety, headaches, loss of appetite, phobias, stiffness and soreness, sinus pain, confusion, diarrhea or constipation, dizziness, loss of reality, blurred vision, emotional outbursts, anger and rage, slurred speech, lack of coordination, muscle spasms, memory impairment, personality changes, sore or achy joints, and emotional exhaustion.

Withdrawal symptoms can range in severity and intensity from mild anxiety, irritability, and craving for the addicting substances to blackouts and seizures, although the latter are rare. Successfully coping with withdrawal and breaking your addiction depends on:

1. *General health and age.* Younger people commonly have "newer" habits. In addition, they are more resilient and generally have more physical resources to draw on.

2. *Psychological stress load and mental state.* Prerequisites for any successful withdrawal are a positive attitude and freedom from tension.

3. *Length of time of addiction.* Generally, the shorter the addiction, the easier it is to break.

4. *Nature of the substance* to which an individual is addicted.

5. *Dosage or concentration* of the addicted substance or

medication, the spacing of dosages and route of administration.
6. *Availability and extent of medical care,* support groups, and family assistance, if needed, that can be expected.
7. *Whether the addiction is part of a peer group milieu.* Often these "friends" can contribute to the problem by peer pressure and the addict's need to fit in.
8. *Personal habits,* including the use of other drugs, medications, or alcohol. In order to have an effective recovery, the amount of chemicals in the body must be reduced.

Recovery Time

The supreme hurdle most people face when detoxing from habit-forming substances is not giving up and feeling helpless and hopeless. Do not become impatient, for it will take the body time to clean itself out of all the chemicals, toxins, and poisons and return to a normal homeostasis.

In recovery, the benzodiazepines and tranquilizers take the biggest toll on your brain and body. They cause physical dependence as well as psychological dependence—more so than do alcohol, cocaine, or heroin.

The number one question for those going into recovery is, "How long will it take before I am free?" Each person is biochemically unique, so the answer depends on your own biological makeup and the condition of your immune system. For some, recovery could take only weeks, others months, but with some it could be a year or more before all of the adverse symptoms are completely gone. Symptoms in the later months will not be as severe as in the beginning, but there are some nagging effects that can linger.

At first, coping with stressful situations may not be easy after withdrawal is begun. Stress and anxiety at the time will be eased by the use of amino acids such as GABA, tyrosine, glutamine, lysine, methionine, vitamin B6 (pyridoxine), and magnesium. The immune system must be restored and constant positive reinforcement given by a therapist.

Freedom from Pills

After taking tranquilizers, pain pills, or antidepressants for a long period, an individual can experience some or all of the following symptoms:

1. Increased anxiety attacks
2. Panic attacks
3. Depression
4. Personality changes
5. Skin and hair problems
6. Glazed eyes

7. Memory problems
8. Digestive upsets
9. Headaches
10. Constant pain
11. Sleep disorders
12. Weight loss or gain
13. Slow reaction time
14. No interest in sex

When a person has a chemical dependency, they cannot just stop. A regular reduction plan must be followed, along with a complete amino acid and nutrient therapy program, as well as a counseling program. This kind of treatment screens the body and brain from feeling severe symptoms, such as sudden drops in the level of the drug in the bloodstream.

The chronic abuse of psychoactive drugs usually leads to what has been termed psychological or psychic dependence. Your attitude and the intensity of your habit, how often you need and use a particular substance, such as tranquilizers or antidepressants, are all aspects which need analysis to aid in your recovery. Those with chronic abuse syndrome not only have psychological dependence, but also an obsession which affects their emotional makeup, mind, and life-style.

Guilt should never influence recovery; if you have had an anxiety or depression problem and were given these medications by a physician, you were following what you thought was a therapeutic dose. *However, when a drug has been taken continuously for more than 4 to 6 months, it has little therapeutic effect on the original symptoms.* The user may only be avoiding withdrawal symptoms by continuing the medication, and he still suffers the toxic effects of the drug.

Just as guilt is a significant factor, so is fear. Constant reinforcement is needed so that fear does not impede recovery. Behavior therapists are of great assistance in substance abuse. They give constant reassurance to aid you in succeeding. Weekly sessions are the best, if possible. A physician or health care professional should be consulted regarding a detox program; if he sees a problem, specific instructions should be given to the patient to prepare him. Careful attention should be given to the complete withdrawal of such drugs in an elderly dependent person, and it should be done only under the supervision of a physician or qualified health care professional.

The speed at which withdrawal is accomplished from any substance depends on what is happening in your life. If you have to operate machinery, drive, have small children, have a stressful job or have a sick person dependent on you, then withdrawal must be done slowly.

Withdrawal Table

Benzodiazepines-Valium (Diazepam 18 mg (2 mg tablets)

Week	Morning	Lunch	Evening		Total	Mg Total
1.	2.5 tabs	2.5 tabs	2.5 tabs	=	7.5 tabs	15 mg
2.	2.0 tabs	2.0 tabs	2.0 tabs	=	6.0 tabs	12 mg
3.	1.5 tabs	1.5 tabs	1.5 tabs	=	4.5 tabs	9 mg
4.	1.0 tab	1.0 tab	1.0 tab	=	3.0 tabs	6 mg
5.	.5 tab	.5 tab	.5 tab	=	1.5 tabs	3 mg

THIS SCHEDULE CAN BE USED FOR WITHDRAWAL FROM MOST OF THE BENODIAZEPINES.
Reduce Only ¼th Of The Daily Dosage Per 7 Days!

Xanax Taper

Example: Patient taking 3 mg of Alprazolam (Xanax) per day.

Week Number	Dose per Day (mg)	Week Number	Dose per Day (mg)
1	2.75	7	1.25
2	2.50	8	1.00
3	2.25	9	0.75
4	2.00	10	0.50
5	1.75	11	0.25
6	1.50	12	Off

Source: *Psychiatric Annals*, March 1995

Phenobarbital Withdrawal Conversion For Benzodiazepines		
Benzodiazepine	Dose (mg)	Phenobarbital Withdrawal Conversion (mg)
Alprazolam (Xanax)	0.5-1.0	30
Chlordiazepoxide (Librium)	25	30
Clonazepam (Klonopin)	2	30
Chlorazepate (Tranxene)	15	30
Diazepam (Valium)	10	30
Flurazepam (Dalmane)	30	30
Lorazepam (Ativan)	2	30
Temazepam (Restoril)	15	30
Triazolam (Halcion)	0.25-0.50	30
Quazepam (Doral)	15	30
Estazolam (ProSom)	2	30

Source: *Psychiatric Annals*, March 1995

Reduction Procedures

Some doctors may recommend hospitalization for withdrawal following a planned program, but many people achieve withdrawal very well at home. If a physician agrees reduction should take place, but fails to recommend a detox schedule, the drug detoxification handbooks used in most psychiatric hospitals recommend a dose reduction of ¼th **the daily dose per 7 days.** (Never compare the number of milligrams; 1 mg of one drug cannot be substituted for 1 mg of another drug. For example, 5 mg of Valium does not equal 5 mg of Halcion or 5 mg of Ativan.)

The body and brain cry and scream wildly at the anticipation of a reduction or not receiving the drugs or substance they are accustomed to receiving. Considering what drugs are suppose to do—for example, relax muscles, control anxiety, or aid sleep—it is understandable that the body and mind object after they have become accustomed to having it present. The rebound reaction, i.e., the opposite of the desired effect, occurs in many people, at least for a period of withdrawal. In the following list of withdrawal symptoms, note that some people may only experience a few of them, especially if they withdraw slowly and use nutrient replacement therapy.

Withdrawal Symptoms by Addictive Substance

Medications:
(For Anxiety, Depression, Pain, Sleep, Hyperactivity and Fear)
Weight loss, chills, hiccups, low back pain, muscle twitching, muscle weakness, tremors, weakness, apathy, craving for the medication/substance, delirium, depression, dizziness, fatigue, insomnia, irritability, loss of appetite, nightmares, panic, anger, rage, crawling sensations on skin, seizures, gooseflesh, rashes, incontinence, stomachaches, intestinal cramps, nausea and vomiting, diarrhea, constipation, yawning, bad taste in mouth, aching in ears, runny nose, smelling of unpleasant odors, watery eyes, uncontrolled blinking, rapid movement of the eyes, dilated pupils, double vision, headaches, muscle contraction headaches, increased anxiety, panic or anxiety attacks, agoraphobia, flu-like symptoms, hyperactivity, hallucinations, confusion, sweating, palpitations, slow or rapid pulse, tight chest, abdominal pain, restlessness, increased sensitivity to noise, light, touch, or smell, change in sex interest, impotence, pains in the shoulder, neck, jaw, or face, jitteriness, and shaking.

Cocaine: Irritability, runny nose, nasal tissue irritation, weight loss or gain, muscle aches, muscle twitching, muscular weakness, anxiety, apathy, craving for cocaine, delirium, depression, fatigue, paranoia, hallucinations, inability to concentrate, insomnia, hyperactivity, nightmares.

Alcohol: Anxiety, craving for addictive substance, delirium, depression, dizziness, fatigue, hallucinations, loss of appetite, hyperactivity, inability to concentrate, insomnia, temporary insanity, tension, unsteady gait, chills, dehydration, fever and sweating, muscle weakness, tremors, weakness, dilated pupils, rapid side-to-side movement of eyeballs, dry

Caffeine:	mouth, nausea, and vomiting. Irritability, muscle contraction headaches, migraine headaches, runny nose, tinnitus (ringing in the ears), rapid pulse, diarrhea, flushing, stomachaches, cramps, urinary frequency, flushing, apathy, craving for coffee, delirium, depression, drowsiness, inability to concentrate, tension, unsteady gait, chills, fever and sweating, tremors, weakness.
Marijuana:	Anxiety, hyperactivity, loss of appetite, craving for marijuana, delirium, depression, drowsiness, insomnia, irritability.
Nicotine:	Weight gain, muscle aches, craving for cigarettes/nicotine, delirium, depression, drowsiness, irritability, insomnia, diarrhea, sore gums or tongue, constipation, stomachaches, intestinal cramping, muscle contraction headaches.
Sugar:	Anxiety, craving for sugar, delirium, rage, depression, dizziness, hyperactivity, inability to concentrate, irritability, anger, tremors, weakness, muscle contraction headaches, blurred vision, rapid heartbeat.
Heroin:	Anxiety, runny nose, dilated pupils, irritability, disturbed sleep, cramps, diarrhea, cramps, vomiting, shaking chills, profuse sweating, sleep disturbances, aches and pains.
Barbiturates:	Anxiety, sleep disturbances, irritability, restlessness, postural hypotension, delirium, major motor seizures, fever.

All withdrawal symptoms pass in time. Knowledge and acceptance of the withdrawal symptoms can shorten the recovery time. The goal of physical and mental well-being represents a state that an addicted person may not have experienced for many years.

Anxiety

The majority of withdrawal symptoms are due to manifestations of anxiety. This does not mean simply worrying about the weather, but disabling physical and emotional symptoms which prevent the sufferer from leading a normal life. Studies have verified that anxiety levels after drugs have been stopped can be six times greater than pre-withdrawal levels; this is known as rebound anxiety.

Tranquilizers make those who are taking them feel as though that part of the brain that deals with anxiety has stopped functioning properly, but it does function at an accelerated rate day and night. The feeling of acceleration is a temporary sensation, and with time it passes.

Drugs may act by stimulating or depressing the normal physiological function of specific organs. Stimulation is an increase in the rate of functional activity of a cell or in the amount of secretion from a gland. Depression denotes a reduction in such activity. Amphetamine and caffeine stimulate the central nervous system, whereas alcohol and phenobarbital depress the brain.

Drugs cannot endow a tissue or cell with properties they do not inherently possess. Thus, no drug is capable of stimulating the epithelial cells located in the mouth to release insulin. A drug cannot transform a muscle fiber in such a manner that it functions as a nerve cell. Drugs can stimulate or depress the normal activity of a nerve or muscle cell. In addition, stimulants such as amphetamines possess a biphasic activity...that is, in moderate doses amphetamines cause *stimulation*, but at higher doses they cause depression. Drugs are unable to restore diseased organs or tissue functions to normal by a direct action.

Neurotransmitters are the chemical language of the brain. These neurotransmitters and endorphins must be produced by the brain for normal functioning during withdrawal. It takes time for the brain's receptor sites to be restored to their normal pattern. Knowledge is power: you need to understand these processes and know that the capability is there to control anxious messages, stress, and depression, and give the brain time to recover.

Grief Reactions

Those going through bereavement are often offered tranquilizers, "to help you get through the tough time." Not only do you run a risk of dependence, but because the drug dulls the emotions you are unable to adjust to the loss or altered situation. You have to face the grief again when the medication ceases, and you may even feel severe guilt about not facing your loss, not having been able to say good-bye or grieve at the "proper" time. In later years, suppressed emotions can come to the surface and cause withdrawal, depression, and delayed grief. As suppressed emotions are released, old fears, phobias, guilts, and anxiety are resolved, and self-respect is regained. It is then that most people are finally able to face old conflicts, traumas, and unresolved anxieties.

Stress Reactions

The key to controlling stress reaction is to conquer the stressors which cause the limbic system in the brain to fire constant messages at the cortex, the reasoning part of the brain. During stress and physical illness, this mechanism may become overstimulated, and the constant anxiety causes an imbalance in the brain's chemistry. Feelings that accompany stress are rapid heart beat, churning stomach, shaking, sweating, feeling of unreality, blurred vision, fear of not being able to get help in time, and fear of death.

The number one stressor in the world today is *uncertainty,* and drugs cannot solve this problem for you. Uncertainty comes when we feel a loss of control in our lives. Posttraumatic stress is often a major factor—we are playing old tapes of painful events in our past; we are fearful of the future, and still enduring grief over events in the past. With help we can put a face on the fear, let time pass, and use relaxation/deep breathing, amino acids, and nutrients to restore an oversensitive nervous system, brain, and body.

Many withdrawal symptoms are due to rebound anxiety according to the *Oxford Textbook of Psychiatry*. Anxiety neuroses have both physical and psychological symptoms. The psychological symptoms include fearful anticipation, irritability, difficulty in concentrating, sensitivity to noise, and a feeling of restlessness. Patients often complain of poor memory, probably due to lack of concentration.

Repetitious thoughts make up an important part of anxiety neuroses. These are often provoked by awareness of the autonomic over-activity; for example, a patient feels his heart beating fast or pounding in his chest and may fear a heart attack. Thoughts of this kind will probably prolong the condition.

The appearance of someone with anxiety neurosis is distinctive. His face appears strained, with a furrowed brow; he is restless and frequently shaky; his posture is tense, his skin looks pale, and often he will sweat from his hands, feet, and armpits. There is also increased tension in the skeletal muscles or over-stimulation of the sympathetic nervous system.

The list of symptoms is extensive and is grouped according to systems in the body:

Symptoms related to the *gastrointestinal system* include rumbling of intestinal gases, frequent or loose bowel movements, excessive air swallowing, epigastric pain (under sternum or breastbone), dry mouth, and feelings of "butterflies" in the stomach.

Cardiovascular symptoms include palpitations, an awareness of missed or irregular heartbeats, throbbing in the neck, feeling of discomfort or pain over the heart or chest, increased or rapid pulse.

Common *respiratory* symptoms include hyperventilation, a feeling of constriction in the chest, and difficulty in catching the breath.

Genitourinary symptoms are increased frequency and urgency of urination, failure of erection, and lack of sexual interest. Women may complain of increased menstrual discomfort or difficulty, and sometimes absence of menstruation.

Other complaints related to the functions of the central nervous system including ringing in the ears, dizziness, prickling sensations, blurred vision, muscular tension in back and shoulders; sleep disturbances such as insomnia, then intermittent awakening, and unpleasant dreams; depersonalization, not feeling in touch with reality, lack of concentration, memory loss, and panic attacks.

Medication Withdrawal Procedure

It is important to learn all that you can about any drug you are taking. Check with your pharmacist, physician, *Physician's Desk Reference* or other reference books on the medication or drug. ***Ask questions. DO NOT be intimidated.***

You can begin by gathering the following information:
1. Determine how addictive the drug is.
2. Determine if **YOU** are addicted. You are if:
   a) Missing even one dosage makes you feel sick, nervous, sad, or you experience a craving for the drug.
   b) You need the drug to function normally.
   c) You begin to require a larger dosage to obtain the same effect.
   d) You continue to use the drug in spite of side effects or other negative reactions.
   e) There is a family history of alcohol or substance abuse.
3. Observe in yourself the withdrawal effects for rapid and slow withdrawal.
4. How long do the withdrawal symptoms last?
5. Can these withdrawal symptoms be minimized without using other medications?

Never stop using a prescription medication unless you have strong feelings and reasons to believe it is harmful to you. Some physicians may not understand your reason for stopping the medication and may feel that you are trying to be an uncooperative patient. They might not support your need to stop and will reassure you that the drug is safe for you for whatever duration you want to take it. But remember that it is *your* body, and the prescription may not always be in your best interest. Don't hesitate to get a second or third opinion from doctors of different orientations and then make your decision based on this information. Drug therapy is a valid medical procedure, but for the most part it is a temporary measure, and to be used only when there is no alternative.

If you decide to quit the drug, know what the withdrawal symptoms are **before** withdrawing. Determine your method and schedule of withdrawal with a physician or qualified health care professional if possible. If your dependency is minor, it probably can be done at home. If your dependency is major, you may need to be in a medical facility for close medical supervision. Be aware that many facilities and physicians use other drugs to withdraw from different substances. *The worst possible treatment is substituting one drug or chemical for another.*

Once your withdrawal effects have been overcome, the next step is to remain off the offending drug or substance. Explore amino acid therapy, and add biofeedback, meditation, homeopathic formulas, phenolics (the neutralization of toxic reactions), herbology (the study and application of herbs), and acupuncture to remain free of the substance. Form new habits and friends by joining Alcoholics Anonymous or Narcotics Anonymous or Palmer Group; these are great support groups and all of the members have had a problem at one time or another. Take one day at a time. Keep alert; become an informed educated consumer; know what you are putting into your body. Ask questions. Do not take any medication unless you know why it is being given to you and what it will do in your body and mind.

3

ALCOHOLISM AND ITS TREATMENT

There are over 100 million people in the United States who drink alcohol. Of these, over 10 million are alcoholics. Alcoholism is ranked the number two killer in this country behind cancer. Many experts believe alcoholism actually outranks cancer as our number one killer. Alcoholism is commonly the "undiagnosed" cause of death. The cost to the economy approaches $50 billion every year!

While there is no one "personality" of an alcoholic, in 1974 Doctors Hague and Howard reported that alcoholics reacted to stress differently than did a nondrinker control group. Changes in eating and sleeping habits and changes in vacations and holidays, divorce, a death in the family, or a job loss caused the alcoholic to feel more stress than a nonalcoholic. Specific personality traits may become more prominent or result in bizarre transformations. The introvert may become extroverted, the gentle one violent, the sensitive one insensitive, and so on. In the early stages, an alcoholic is often irritable, very moody, and depressed when he is not drinking. He denies that he is drinking too much, blaming his drinking on his wife, his job, stress, etc.

An alcoholic sees the world around him as close, threatening, and anxiety-producing. The alcoholic uses alcohol to solve his problems because these scary feelings disappear after a drink—his blood alcohol increases and the self-degenerating circuits of the brain are anesthetized. The alcohol is a way of acknowledging or dealing with depression as it gives a temporary lift and relief from the depression, but the relief is short-lived because alcohol is a central nervous system depressant. After the high wears off the depression may intensify. So the addiction goes on and on.

Alcohol shares many similar properties with the hypnotic and antianxiety drugs. Alcohol seems to serve as courage for the alcoholic since it works primarily on anticipatory anxiety. The alcoholic is in a state of chronic anxiety. As a side note, alcohol has been shown to operate as an MAO inhibitor, which is a category of antidepressant.

Progression Of Drinking Symptoms

Development Stage	Overt Alcoholism	Deterioration Stage
Social drinking	Loss of control	Vague fears
Once a week	Before breakfast	Prefers solitary life
Drinking faster than associates	Protects supply	Delirium tremors
Drinking more than associates	Weekends lost	Insomnia
Blackouts (memory)	Solitary drinking	Loss or depletion of vitamin stores
More drunk than associates	Will not share thinking or ideas	Depletion of mineral stores
Avoidance of family closeness	Decreased tolererance	Death

Symptoms Of Alcohol Withdrawal
(Mild Or Early)

Behavior Changes
  Irritability
  Restlessness
  Agitation
  Hostility
  Exaggerated startle response

Sleep Disturbances
  Insomnia
  Restless sleep
  Nightmares

Impaired Cognitive Function
  Easily distracted
  Impairment of memory
  Inability to concentrate
  Impairment of judgment and other mental functions

Gastrointestinal Problems
  Appetite loss
  Nausea
  Vomiting
  Abdominal discomfort
  Diarrhea

Muscular Symptoms
  Cramps
  Weakness
  Trembling

Autonomic Imbalances
  Tachycardia or rapid heart beat >100 beats/minute
  Systolic hypertension (high blood pressure)
  Shakiness
  Fever
  Sweating or diaphoresis

Symptoms Of Alcohol Withdrawal
(Late Or Severe)

Worsening of mild symptoms of alcohol withdrawal
- Tremor
- Tachycardia
- Agitation
- Diaphoresis
- Marked startle response

Delusions
- Paranoia
- Mixed with and reinforced by hallucinations
- Can create agitation and terror

Delirium
- Changes from one hour to the next in severity and nature
- Impairment of thinking
- Disorientation as to time and place
- Clouding of senses

Hallucinations
- Can be visual, auditory, or tactile
- Can be threatening in nature

Seizures
- Usually generalized and nonfocal
- History of prior seizure disorder not necessary
- Usually occurs within 48 hours after cessation of drinking
- Usually self-limiting
- Always precede severe delirium, agitation, and hallucinations.

All mammals, including humans, make a small amount of alcohol in the body as part of normal metabolism. In this process the average person makes about one ounce of alcohol per day, which is broken down in the liver by an enzyme called alcohol dehydrogenase. This enzyme also handles the alcohol ingested from alcoholic beverages.

In the next step, alcohol is converted by alcohol dehydrogenase to acetaldehyde, and this substance can damage the body in several ways:

1. It can cause abnormal chemical bonds in large molecules like proteins (causing hardening of the arteries, loss of elasticity, skin wrinkling).
2. It can damage the DNA molecule (resulting in abnormal cell function.
3. Damage can also result when acetaldehyde is oxidized in the body, yielding dangerous and reactive chemical fragments called free radicals; these can cause damage to many cell structures, cancer, birth defects, atherosclerosis, and are implicated as major factors in aging.

****

METABOLISM OF ALCOHOL

Alcohol------------→ alcohol dehydrogenase------→ acetaldehyde
acetaldehyde------→ aldehydrogenase--------------→ acetate
                                                    (common vinegar)
Acetate-------------→ carbon dioxide + water

****

The acetaldehyde is a very toxic chemical, and the body breaks it down by the enzyme called aldehyde dehydrogenase; this is a most crucial breakdown. If the liver does not produce enough aldehyde dehydrogenase many toxic side effects can occur, especially to the liver cells. "Normal" people who do not ingest excess alcohol have no difficulty breaking down the alcohol to acetate in their bodies. The enzyme system can be overloaded when alcohol is ingested too quickly. Acetaldehyde and its free radical by-products from the alcohol breakdown cause most of the damage to the body and the brain, including cardiovascular disease, premature aging, liver damage, brain damage, lowered resistance to disease, alcohol addiction, etc.

In the brain an overload of acetaldehyde can lead to bizarre and complicated chemical reactions. It competes with other chemical substances known as brain amines or neurotransmitters for the attention of certain enzymes. Acetaldehyde blocks the enzymes from achieving their primary duty of inhibiting the neurotransmitter activity. Addiction to alcohol might never occur if acetaldehyde stopped interfering at this point with the brain's chemical activities. The brain neurotransmitters interact with acetaldehyde to form compounds called *isoquinolines*. These compounds also release the stored neurotransmitters. The isoquinolines are very similar to the opiates, and research has suggested that they may act on the opiate receptors in the brain. The opiate receptors may contribute to the addiction of alcohol. These mischievous substances may trigger the alcoholic to drink more and more to counter the painful effects of the increasing buildup of acetaldehyde.

Recently scientists have discovered that many alcoholics have a metabolic defect which causes them to have twice as much of the toxic acetaldehyde in their bloodstream after a drink as normal people. This is enough to set the vicious cycle into motion. Acetaldehyde made by the liver makes the drinker feel bad so he drinks more alcohol; this makes him feel better and helps to protect him from the acetaldehyde poison—until the liver produces more acetaldehyde out of the additional alcohol, so he indulges and has some more drinks, and on and on goes the cycle.

Researchers have looked and continue to look for the *one* cause of alcoholism. But all research has concluded that there is no one factor; studies have shown that a number of physiological differences exist between the nonalcoholic and the alcoholic. Physiology determines whether one person becomes alcoholic and another does not. The alcoholic's body—his hormones, enzymes, genes, and brain chemistry—all work jointly to cause his abnormal reaction to alcohol. Of course, psychological, family history, and social factors certainly influence the alcoholic's drinking habits and behavior.

Alcoholism and nutrition are interrelated and intertwined on many levels:

1. Ethyl alcohol, or ethanol, itself contains nutrients; however, it also changes the balance of other nutrients in the diet and may disperse them as well.
2. The absorption and digestion of many nutrients is affected by the ingestion of ethanol; it may alter dietary requirements.
3. In addiction, nutritional alterations may affect the metabolism of alcohol in the body.
4. Chronic alcohol consumption may cause temporary or permanent damage to many organs—the liver, brain, heart, and bone marrow. The effects may be modified by nutritional factors such as dietary intake of protein, fat, and vitamins.
5. Organ damage may yield changes in nutrient metabolism. The organ most affected is the liver. The liver plays an important role in metabolism and is frequently altered with alcohol ingestion.

Identifying the cause of malnutrition in alcoholism is not a simple matter. Certain groups of alcoholics may have an inadequate nutrient intake, but a major factor is the primary toxic effect of ethanol on the gastrointestinal tract, pancreas, liver, bone marrow, and other tissues such as the heart. Research data by Rubin and Lieber in 1974 suggested that a nutritious diet could not and will not prevent the development of alcoholic liver disease.

Factors Leading To Malnutrition In Alcoholism

1. Decreased or sporadic food ingestion
    Intoxication
    Poverty and economic factors
    Abnormal appetite

Anorexia
Mental illness/disease

2. Increased nutrient losses
Urinary
Toxic effects of alcohol on the kidneys
Fecal
   a) Malabsorption due to GI effects of alcohol
   b) Maldigestion due to inflamed pancreas

3. Reduced or deficient nutrient stores
Decreased uptake of nutrients
Alcoholic hepatitis
Cirrhosis (inflammation of liver)
Reduced nutrient intake
Increased inactivation of vitamins and nutrients

4. Impaired nutrient utilization due to defective metabolism
Alcoholic liver disease
Toxic effects of alcohol on bone marrow

Alcoholic beverages provide mainly calories which are derived from their ethanol content. A pint of 86 proof liquor supplies about half the normal daily calories required by an adult, but these alcoholic calories are utterly empty of other nutrients. Ethanol does not even provide caloric food value equal to carbohydrates. If alcohol consumption is heavy and the drinker limits his food intake, he worsens his already severe vitamin and nutrient deficiencies. Conversely, if he does *not* reduce his food intake, many of the extra ethanol calories are converted to fat, causing high serum triglyceride levels and obesity.

Acute and chronic consumption of alcohol may markedly alter digestion and gastrointestinal absorption. Alcohol-induced changes in digestion and absorption may yield marginal deficiencies or augment deficiencies arising from other causes.

A number of neurological syndromes occurring with the chronic usage of alcohol are attributed to vitamin deficiencies. Just to name a few, these include: Wernicke's disease, Korsakoff's syndrome, peripheral neuropathy, Morel's carotid sclerosis, and cellular degeneration. Alterations in the metabolism of the B vitamins in the alcoholic person affect the levels in his body. Commonly, the level of B1 (thiamine), B3 (niacin), B6 (pyridoxine), B12, B15, and folic acid are decreased in the alcoholic. Anemias are seen with deficiencies of folic acid or B6 while deficiencies of niacin or thiamine may cause neurological symptoms.

Alcohol/Drug-Induced Nutritional Deficiencies

Vitamins Depleted	Minerals Depleted
Folic acid	Magnesium
Thiamine	Zinc
Niacin	
Riboflavin	
Ascorbic acid (Vitamin C)	
Vitamin B6	
Vitamin B12	

The metabolism of the fat-soluble vitamins may be altered due to the alcohol ingestion. In alcoholics with cirrhosis, vitamin A deficiencies may occur; this is due to malabsorption, impaired liver storage of vitamin A, or to simply too much alcohol in the body competing in the liver. Vitamin D may be depleted through dietary insufficiency. Vitamin K deficiency in the alcoholic may manifest itself as a bleeding disorder related to the liver's failure to make clotting factors.

Mineral deficiencies can be caused by alcohol, especially magnesium and zinc; alcohol increases the excretion of magnesium and zinc via the kidneys. Magnesium depletion can be responsible for the symptoms of the "horror" or delirium tremors. Low levels of calcium have been found due to increased excretion of calcium in the urine over a period of years; this can lead to osteoporosis.

The excessive intake of alcohol is one factor which precipitates clinical vitamin deficiencies. This depletion usually includes many of the vitamins, but the most common are: folic acid, thiamine, riboflavin, niacin, B6, B12, and vitamin C. Mineral depletion usually includes magnesium and zinc. A protein deficiency usually exists due to malnutrition. The alcoholic has a wide range of deficiencies and needs nutritional supplementation.

Treatment

Treatment for and control of the ingestion of alcohol requires a team effort. Good nutrition can help in the control by maintaining an adequate blood sugar level. Dr. Robert Meiers has found a low blood sugar level (hypoglycemia) in 95% of alcoholics; this results from the lack of food intake and substituting alcohol for essential calories and nutrients. Hypoglycemia has been implicated as one of the contributing factors in the cause of alcoholism. If the blood sugar drops, the alcoholic needs a drink. Blood sugar can be controlled by taking chromium picolinate 400 mcg daily helps to normalize blood sugar. Chromium picolinate is known as the glucose tolerance mineral.

Abstinence is the ultimate goal. The greatest majority of alcoholics cannot become social drinkers again because they tend to relapse into heavy drinking. In *Feed Yourself Right* by Lendon Smith, M.D., he states, "All people who drink must remember that alcohol is a biochemical stress, and each swallow must be accompanied with B vitamins, some nourishing food, and at least sometime that day or week, the minerals known to be lost must be replaced."

Nutrient and Amino Acid Program for the Therapeutic Treatment of Alcoholism

Please note the following supplements should be taken on a daily basis to maintain brain chemistry and control craving.

Brain Link Neurotransmitter formula	1 scoop three times daily morning, afternoon and evening.
Calcium 1,000 mg Magnesium 500 mg and Zinc 25 mg	**This is in one formula:** Cal-Mag-Zinc 3 at bedtime
Esterfied C	1,000 mg in the morning and evening
DLPA	2 capsules with each meal
Pyridoxine (B6) 5 mg	1 time released in the morning
GABA 750	1/2 capsule in water in morning and afternoon
Anxiety Formula	2 capsules as needed for anxiety or craving daily. Up to 6 capsules daily.
Super Glutamine Powder	1,000 mg per scoop. Can be used with a Total Vite in place of Brain Link if preferred.

This same program is used for cocaine and other recreational drugs in the same dosages. This program can be used as long as necessary.

We would like to mention here, and strongly recommend that if you have an alcohol or substance abuse problem, you seek out a psychotherapist or behavior therapist that you can work with and get counseling for yourself and your family. If you are the child of an alcoholic you are predisposed to an addictive personality and should seek counseling.

Children of alcoholics have the same neurotransmitter imbalances as their parents or even grandparents. The deficiencies can show up in many ways such as A.D.D. This means the child has a glutamine deficiency that must be corrected. Use Brain Link daily and Super Glutamine powder 1,000 to 3,000 mgs daily as needed. If anxiety is a problem use Anxiety Control; if under 75 lbs. take 1 capsule or if over 75 lbs. take 2 capsules 2 times daily. Many teachers will suggest Ritalin; do not think this is the answer, it is not. Address deficiencies in the brain with Brain Link and glutamine. Ritalin is addictive and is not the answer for children of alcoholics. Memory and concentration problems are commonly associated not only with alcoholics but children of alcoholics.

4
NICOTINE AND CAFFEINE ADDICTION AND TREATMENT

Nicotine

Although the number of smokers in the United States has decreased, approximately one-fourth of the population continues to smoke or use nicotine in some form. Nicotine is an oily poisonous liquid found only in the tobacco plant. Pharmaceutically, it is characterized as an organic nerve drug; it is so powerful that one drop injected in a human can cause instant death.

Four types of smoking dependency have been identified by Karl-Olov Fagerstrom of Sweden:

Type 1 is the social smoker. He smokes for image, using it as a way of relieving tension and giving him something to do with his hands.

Type 2 is the person whose smoking habit evolves around daily activities such as breaks, meals, telephone calls, etc., as well as social functions.

Type 3 is one who is chemically or emotionally dependent on nicotine; he is "hooked" on it. This person smokes all day long, from just awakening until bedtime. A certain plasma level of nicotine must be maintained or he will experience withdrawal symptoms.

Type 4 has a psychological and chemical dependency. He smokes more heavily and inhales more deeply than Type 3.

Tobacco smoking depletes the body of Vitamins A, B1 (Thiamine), B5 (Pantothenic Acid), B6 (Pyridoxine), C, and E. The amino acid cysteine is also depleted. Every cigarette burns about 25 mg of Vitamin C—possibly one of the reasons smokers generally look older than their nonsmoking counterparts. These deficiencies may contribute to mood swings and possibly depression. Tyrosine, an amino acid, can be very helpful as a mood elevator. Doses of 850 mg or 1,000 mg a day will raise the body's norepinephrine levels, the mood elevating neurotransmitter that helps to break through the stress and depression that comes when you begin to decrease nicotine.

Nicotine readily crosses the blood-brain barrier. It is distributed throughout the brain, and its uptake appears to involve both passive diffusion and active transport. Within the brain, the specific binding of nicotine is greatest in the hypothalamus, hippocampus, thalamus, midbrain, and brain stem, as well as in areas of the cerebral cortex.

Short-term exposure to nicotine results in the activation of several central nervous system neurohormonal pathways resulting in the release of acetylcholine, norepinephrine, dopamine, serotonin, vasopressin, growth hormone, and ACTH.

Most of the effects of nicotine on the central nervous system are due to direct actions on brain receptors. Nicotine causes the release of catecholamines and facilitates the release of neurotransmitters from sympathetic nerves in blood vessels. Stimulation of the sympathetic nervous system results in an increased heart rate and blood pressure while the blood flow to the extremities decreases due to constriction of blood vessels.

Nicotine freely crosses the placenta and has been found in amniotic fluid and umbilical cord blood in newborns. Additionally, it is found in breast milk.

Nicotine Withdrawal Program

Make a decision that you are going to quit. *Today you have become a nonsmoker.* Put your heart into the decision, and mean it 100%. Decide whether to quit slowly or rapidly. There are advantages to both, so you must decide what is best for you. Some people like to slowly taper down on their cigarette/nicotine habit; others find quitting "cold turkey" is the best way to handle the habit. When you taper down, the nicotine commonly causes a craving in the brain for more. It is as though you have a full tank and when your gas tank (your brain and body) starts noticing a decrease in the level of nicotine your body wants to replenish that level to full, so you crave nicotine.

If you decide to quit slowly, set a target date a month in advance. Ask your family and friends to reinforce your decision by supporting you. Invite a friend to also quit. Keep a journal of each day during the 4 weeks, noting the exact time of every cigarette that you smoke and why. Decrease usage. You might try delaying each cigarette that you smoke by 5 minutes the first day, 6 minutes the second, and so forth until you have quit. Change to a brand that you dislike. Change hands from the hand you normally use with a cigarette. Using aversion therapy such as imagining that the cigarettes taste like the smell of the ashes or imagining that the cigarettes taste just as bad as the first time you put one to your mouth, works well for some people. On the day you quit, throw all your cigarettes away. Get rid of ashtrays, matches, etc.

Conversely, if you quit quickly or cold turkey, you may experience withdrawal symptoms, but many people find this is the best way. The nicotine is out of the system in 24 hours, but the craving may continue for 72 hours. Many people experience withdrawal symptoms such as irritability, depression, anxiety, headaches, and sleep disorders for the first 72 hours; after 3 days, the craving for nicotine is simply a habit of reaching for a cigarette/nicotine.

But once you stop, think only of yourself as a NON-smoker. If at any time you desire a cigarette, take in a very, very deep breath because your body is actually craving oxygen; this can stop the urge for a cigarette. Sit in the nonsmoking section of restaurants. Increase your vitamin C intake to at least 3,000 mg of Ester C daily–half in the morning and half in the evening. Many people fear gaining weight after they quit smoking. It is true your metabolism does slow down, but only very slightly. You may experience your stomach growling or churning because it has been producing more hydrochloric acid to overcome the nicotine that was swallowed. Some peppermint in the form of tea, gum, or a candy may help quiet the stomach. Watching your diet and food consumption closely can help prevent a weight gain. It takes two to three months for your body to return to its regular metabolic rate after you quit smoking. As a cleaning process, your body flushes fluid into the tissues; this may reinforce the belief that you will gain weight when you quit smoking. It is only temporary, and drinking plenty of water and fluids will help.

The most common problem that smokers experience is what to do with their hands. Stay busy! Pick up a new hobby like exercising, walking, crocheting, knitting, whittling, or cleaning. Remember, it takes 21-25 days to form a new habit.

If you had a habit of smoking a cigarette after meals, change your habit by going for a short walk instead. But **DO NOT** try to also cut down or quit drinking coffee (caffeine) at the same that you are stopping smoking. It will produce too much stress on your system if you experience both nicotine and caffeine withdrawal at the same time. Conquer the nicotine habit first, then the caffeine at a later date.

Probably the next most common problem is irritability, jitteriness, and reaching for a cigarette at the first sign of stress. The one leads to two and before you know it, you are back smoking.

We have successfully used a combination program at the Pain & Stress Center in San Antonio. We use the Anxiety Control 24, GABA 750, Esterified Vitamin C, and nutrients which inhibit the craving for nicotine. Additionally, hypnosis is sometimes employed to assist quitting. Try to decrease your intake of meat, seafood, eggs, and poultry. Eat plenty of fruits and vegetables; these foods help to make your urine more alkaline and help you eliminate the nicotine from your system more quickly. Drink as much water as possible to help flush out nicotine. Use 2 Anxiety Control 24 as needed. Get chewable Ester C and chew a wafer to help decrease craving.

Caffeine

Probably one of the most used drugs in the world is caffeine. It is extremely popular because it is mentally stimulating. It is found in tea, coffee, soft drinks, some over the counter pain pills, and in the herbs. Recently, colas have replaced coffee as the number one source of caffeine intake.

Caffeine belongs to one of the class of chemicals called xanthine. It has several physiological effects including stimulation of the central nervous system, heart, skeletal muscles, kidneys (causing increased urinary output), adrenal glands, and increased rate and depth of respiration. The peak blood level of caffeine occurs one to two hours after consumption, but increased alertness and perception with decreased fatigue occur almost immediately. The average adult gets a lift with 150-250 mg of caffeine. Caffeine is a potent, addicting drug. Stopping caffeine suddenly may cause headaches and other withdrawal symptoms. Greater than 500 mg a day is considered heavy usage.

Caffeine Content Of Various Substances

	Mg/Oz.	8 Oz. Cup	12 Oz.
Drip Coffee	30	240 mg	
Percolated Coffee	22	176 mg	
Instant Coffee	16	128 mg	
Decaffeinated Coffee	1	8 mg	
Decaffeinated, Instant	1/2	4 mg	
Tea	2-10	16-80 mg	
Hot Cocoa	13		
Vivarin (each tablet)	200		
Dexatrim	200		
NoDoz	100		
Excedrin	65		
Midol	30		
Soft Drinks:			
Mountain Dew			50 mg
Diet Pepsi			32 mg
Sunkist Orange			38 mg
Dr. Pepper			37 mg
Coca-Cola			32 mg

Caffeine stimulates the release of norepinephrine and other brain neurotransmitters. This occurs in the brain and body and gives the lift associated with caffeine ingestion. With large long-term caffeine consumption depletion of the neurotransmitters may result unless there is an ample supply of precursors or amino acids for replacement. Without replacement of these neurotransmitters, a caffeine user will begin to feel nervous and fatigued. Caffeine is believed to exert its biochemical effect by locking onto brain receptors producing a "relaxing" chemical called adenosine; this is responsible for the wake-up effect.

Caffeine interferes with the absorption and metabolism of Vitamin B1 or thiamine, thereby effecting our moods. Ingestion of large amounts of caffeine can eventually result in a Vitamin B1 deficiency.

One study showed that 300 mg of caffeine caused a 50 percent increase in the loss of magnesium and a 100 percent increase in the loss of calcium. Caffeine in the form of coffee and tea markedly inhibits iron absorption when taken with a meal or up to one hour following meals. A low iron level can contribute to depression.

Caffeine Detox Procedure

1. Calculate daily caffeine consumption.
2. Keep a journal of how much caffeine is ingested from all sources. Physical dependency can occur on 5 or more cups per day.
3. Gradually taper off, perhaps using a procedure of gradual dilution. Here is a suggested schedule for withdrawal with a coffee mixture:

   Mix 3/4 caffeine coffee and 1/4 decaf for 3-7 days.
   Then 1/2 caffeine coffee and 1/2 decaf for 3-7 days.
   Then 1/4 caffeine coffee and 3/4 decaf for 3-7 days.
   Then decaf.
   Try decaffeinated herbal tea; it will help you relax.

   For soft drinks, simply reduce your intake on a schedule such as the one above.

   For pills/tablets, cut pills into halves or quarters.

Withdraw slowly from caffeine or you will experience unpleasant side effects such as headaches, shakes, stomach cramps, flushing, irritability, tension. Supplementing with tyrosine, Anxiety Control 24, ginseng, and Esterified C may reduce any withdrawal symptoms.

5
AMINO ACIDS FOR THERAPY

Amino acid supplements have a positive effect on people with addictive behavior. Combinations of amino acids have been used to speed the healing of injuries and deficiencies to the body as a result of substance abuse. Amino acids also assist the body in handling the stress of recovery and can be continued to help prevent relapse of addiction.

The vast field of amino acid interactions is just beginning to unfold. For example, many of the amino acids are absorbed and metabolized in a similar fashion, and there is a great deal of competition between molecules; sometimes, one amino acid can cancel the effect of others, or they can inhibit one another's passage into the brain. This usually occurs among amino acids with similar structure. Taurine and glycine have the same function and compete for absorption.

Dietary amino acids will certainly affect the concentration of those neurotransmitters from which they are metabolically derived. So dopamine, norepinephrine, serotonin, histamine, and GABA can be increased or decreased depending upon excesses or deficiencies in their parent amino acids. Amino acid availability can affect the hypothalamus and its functions. A role for amino acids in behavior disorders has been identified; Methionine and its relationship with serotonin, tryptophan, glycine, and leucine is important for schizophrenia, sleep disorders, and affective disorders.

Among the indications with significance for brain function, choline is essential to the absorption of acetylcholine in the brain, and it can be regulated by dietary intake. Glutamine does affect important functions relating to learning and memory and concentration.

Functions of the nervous system depend upon the relationship between nutrients and brain function that will serve as a significant basis for behavioral pharmacological, and metabolic events.

A recent theory published by Richard Bergland, M.D., a neurosurgeon, documents a decade of research which has yielded a modern view of the brain much as the ancient Greeks imagined it—as a hormonally modulated gland. The "stuff of thought," Dr. Bergland argues, is not electricity, as scientists of the last two thousand years have believed, but hormones; every time we move or laugh or cry, hormones spill into our brains, affecting our behavior.

In that respect, the brain shares the same internal composition as the other organs of the body.

The realization that the brain is a gland, controlled by the hormones within it, is less than ten years old. It is suddenly clear that the unraveling of the mysteries of behavior can come through a better understanding of brain hormones. But more than that: many kinds of illnesses, especially those related to stress, anxiety, and depression will be more easily treated by understanding the hormonal signals that move back and forth between the body and the brain. Many scientists believe that when a person goes into a state of extreme rage, the brain is filled with catecholamines either adrenalin, noradrenalin, or serotonin. These could trigger the release of many other hormones, each of which could affect behavior and cloud a person's ability to make sound judgments. Fear, like rage, releases catecholamines and hormones, and the level of amino acids in the brain drops. Many addictive and behavioral diseases may result from a mistuned blood brain barrier that allows the brain to receive too few or too many amino acids.

GABA

Probably the least understood part of the entire limbic system is the ring of cerebral cortex called the limbic cortex. This part functions as a crossover zone where signals are transmitted from the rest of the cortex into the limbic system. The function of the limbic cortex appears to be a link to the cerebral cortex for the control of behavior. Anxiety occurs when the limbic system—the part of the brain that stores anxiety messages—begins to release numerous signals, and, simultaneously, a physiological response starts to take place . . . the fight-or-flight syndrome. To an anxious person, this threatens a potential loss of control.

The unceasing alert signals from the limbic system eventually overwhelm the cortex. Then the ability of the cortex and the rest of the stress network to accommodate the crisis becomes exhausted. The balance between the limbic system and the cortex goes to pieces, often leading people into erratic or irrational fear . . or making them want to reach for their favorite substance.

The ability of the cortex to communicate with the limbic system and the rest of the brain in an orderly fashion depends critically on inhibition, namely GABA (Gamma- Aminobutyric Acid). GABA inhibits the cells from firing, diminishing the excitatory messages reaching the frontal cortex. GABA seems to lower the excitatory level of the cell that is about to receive the incoming information. If the anxiety, stress, or fear continues, GABA's ability to block the messages is decreased, and finally the process by which the signals are rated for priority breaks down and the frontal cortex is literally bombarded with anxiety messages. There follows a full-blown panic attack.

With the limbic system firing broadside fight-or-flight signals at the frontal cortex, the subject's ability to reason is diminished. The effects now can include fear of dying, pounding heart, sweating, trembling, tightness, weakness, loss of control, disorientation—the list is endless. Research has shown that GABA can actually mimic the tranquilizing effect of Valium and Librium but without the heavy sedation effect of these drugs. This information was first released for publication in 1982 in *Life Extension* by Sandy Shaw and Durk Pearson. Since that time, numerous studies have been published showing the successful use of GABA with anxiety-prone individuals and phobics. Many addicts, both drug and alcohol, have a tremendous problem with anxiety and anticipatory fear.

Research reports have shown that a person who constantly experiences "what-if" type anxiety, or what is termed "anticipatory fear", has empty GABA receptors in the brain. This means that the brain can be bombarded with random firings of excitatory messages. It is the receptor site in the brain that prevents the reception of all the random firings so that the brain does not become overwhelmed. In *Lancet*, August 14, 1982, a research report about tranquilizers and GABA transmission clearly stated that GABA is a major inhibitory transmitter in the mammalian central nervous system and that the agents that raise the brain's GABA concentration possess a sedative anticonvulsant property.

After publication of information about GABA, the public quickly became aware of the potentiality of GABA as an anti-anxiety formula. A survey of the medical journals shows over 300 articles (case studies, clinical reports, etc.) on GABA by orthomolecular psychiatrists and researchers.

GABA and the neurons that utilize it as an inhibitory transmitter, is found throughout the central nervous system. In view of the growing knowledge regarding the regulation of the physiology of the central nervous system, GABA is assuming an ever-enlarging role as a major influence on drugs, in many cases replacing them (for example, Valium and Xanax). Preliminary pharmacological and clinical data have already demonstrated the usefulness of GABA in exploring human disease.

As of 1986, clinical research at the Pain & Stress Center in San Antonio using pure GABA 750 mg, demonstrated the effectiveness of GABA as a muscle relaxant as well as an antianxiety agent. Pure GABA is tasteless, odorless, and colorless; it readily dissolves in water. In 100 patient trials done at the Pain & Stress Center, GABA

750 reduced the level of tension in the muscles in 7 to 10 minutes. Additionally, GABA is helpful in reducing anxiety and can help decrease anxiety remarkably. There are GABA receptor sites throughout the body as well as the brain.

Dr. K. J. Berman at Mt. Sinai School of Medicine published an extensive review in *Clinical Neuropharmacology* (1985) entitled "Progabide: A New GABA Mimetric Electric Agent in Clinical Use." Dr. Berman sums up the research and results of the clinical chemistry, the role of GABA, and the influences in the central nervous system. In 1985 the most valid research published on GABA relates to anxiety. In 1988 GABA's benefits are still being explored. GABA not only aids anxiety sufferers, but also lessens muscle tension, and aids Parkinson's symptoms, as well as inhibiting the desire for alcohol and cocaine. Soon this extremely versatile amino acid will make more major contributions to aid those suffering from pain, stress, anxiety, and addiction.

L-Glutamine
The Surprising Brain Fuel

Glutamine, an amino acid found in many foods is the third most abundant in the blood and brain. Glutamine provides a major alternative fuel source for the brain when blood sugar levels are low.

Glutamine is an inhibitory neurotransmitter and is the precursor for GABA, the antianxiety amino acid. Glutamine helps the brain dispose of waste ammonia, which is a protein breakdown by-product and is irritating to brain cells even at low levels. Recent scientific research regarding glutamine demonstrates its link to the most important functions of the body's vital organs and musculoskeletal system. Glutamine aids the body in muscle development when illness causes muscle wasting. This occurs following a high fever, chronic stress, illness or a traumatic accident.

Glutamine's most important function is the immune system. Glutamine is involved with the multiplication of selected white cells, which strengthen the body's defense system. Glutamine aids other immune cells in killing bacteria. Glutamine aids in healing wounds. It supports pancreatic growth. It maintains and supports glutathione, an important antioxidant.

Scientist at NIH in 1970 found glutamine, not glucose, is the most important nutrient for the intestinal tract. During times of illness, the body uses more glutamine to aid in tissue repair in the kidneys, intestines and liver. For many years glutamine was considered a nonessential amino acid, but research the past several years has brought forth a wave of new important information that has changed this view. Everyday more research is being done on the healing power of amino acids.

This amazing amino acid, along with GABA and Glycine, is rapidly becoming the most important therapeutic amino acids of the twenty-first century.

Neurotransmitters in the brain function: The amino acid trio of Glutamine, GABA, Glycine and B-6 the cofactor are the major inhibitory neurotransmitters in the brain. Glutamine is found in the nerves of the hippocampus, the memory center of the brain, in the cranial nerves and in many other areas of the brain. These three amino acids work together and are inhibitory neurotransmitters the chemical language of the brain. Anyone taking amino acids must take B-6 to metabolize the amino acids.

GABA and Glutamine are NOT only found in the brain but in the receptor cites throughout the body. Amino acids can and do change mind, mood, memory and behavior.

For those with alcohol craving Dr. Roger William, pioneer in Glutamine research, found that 3 to 4 thousand milligrams of glutamine daily will stop the craving for alcohol and decrease the craving for sweets. Since glutamine is tasteless and mixes with water or any liquid it is easy to take. Our patients also reported a lift from fatigue both mental and physical. One alcoholic stopped drinking when glutamine was administered daily. Two years later the patient was still alcohol free from the craving for alcohol. He maintained a nutritional support program. Dr. Lorene Rogers, researcher at the University of Texas, Clayton Foundation reported several cases in which glutamine was successful, and placebos ineffective. Glutamine was given to one group of alcoholics and placebos to the other. The group taking at least three thousand milligrams of glutamine daily were free of alcohol craving.

Glutamine is converted to energy by the brain and is its main fuel. It is converted to GABA with the help of magnesium. Without continued high energy in the brain, the rest of the mind and body will NOT function properly. The brain requires a huge supply of glucose and oxygen in order to perform properly. This energy supply is delivered via the bloodstream. Proper circulation ensures the brain will have the energy it needs.

The main nutrient needed for intestinal repair is glutamine. Leaky gut syndrome is being seen more often today due to the increased use of anti-inflammatory medications such as Motrin, Advil, Ibuprofen, Dolobid, Anaprox, Orudis, Naprosyn, etc.

Unfortunately foods are not a good source of glutamine. The foods highest in glutamine include meat, chicken and eggs, but in the RAW form. Cooking or heat inactivates glutamine, so your best source is in supplement form.

Glutamine is truly an amazing amino acid with multiple benefits and with continued research other important factors will be found that will improve our quality of life. Glutamine is available in capsule and powder forms.

Phenylalanine

Currently, ten to fifteen compounds have been identified as neurotransmitters. As far as we know, not all of these neurotransmitters are affected by diet, but three are definitely related to dietary control. These are norepinephrine, acetylcholine and serotonin.

Another amino acid, phenylalanine, is one of the essential amino acids, and it is necessary for life. It is a precursor to norepinephrine; norepinephrine functions both as a stimulatory neurotransmitter and as a brain hormone. The formation of these transmitters is affected by diet, by making more or less of the respective precursors which are available to the brain. The rate that each of these is synthesized is affected by the availability of the particular substance. As a result, the rate of synthesis of serotonin that is immediately available is influenced by how much tryptophan is present. Similarly, the amount of norepinephrine that is available to the brain is predisposed by the amount of amino acid precursors, phenylalanine, and tyrosine.

L-phenylalanine is the raw substance that produces several compounds of the catecholamine family of compounds which are responsible for the transmission of nerve impulses; provided that a good supply of phenylalanine (or tyrosine) is in the blood, the adrenal medulla and the nerve cells can rapidly produce these catecholamines. L-phenylalanine is one of the essential nutrients for life. All of the amino acids are the building blocks of protein, but phenylalanine is one of the few amino acids that is readily converted into the brain compounds that control a person's moods.

Phenylalanine is required in the body to rebuild proteins; its most important role may be in the production of the critical hormones epinephrine (adrenalin), dopa, norepinephrine, dopamine, thyroxine, and tri-iodthyronine. Phenylalanine is found in a variety of foods in small amounts. Inadequate amounts of phenylalanine lead to low levels of norepinephrine which can result in severe depression. Since phenylalanine is converted to tyrosine, dopa, dopamine, norepinephrine, and epinephrine, these compounds are called, as a whole, neurotransmitters. They control the whole basic process of nerve impulse transmission. Epinephrine is important because it is excreted at the nerve terminals in the hypothalamus and norepinephrine is excreted at the sympathetic nerve endings giving a basic fight-or-flight response. Thus it affects the immediate postsynaptic cells.

Norepinephrine is the principal neurotransmitter at the peripheral nerve endings of the sympathetic nervous system; norepinephrine is the neurotransmitter in certain central synapses and is stored in the presynaptic vesicles.

Serotonin Pathways

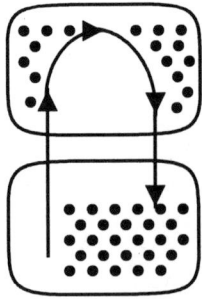

Serotonin released in the brain. It should be recirculated so it can be utilized. Serotonin is made from the amino acid, tryptophan.

Serotonin is blocked in the brain by SSRI's, antidepressants and tricyclics. A person is at risk for Serotonin Syndrome to develop.

Whenever the body is under a tremendous amount of stress, an enormous load is placed on the adrenal glands; many times, the epinephrine and norepinephrine levels—especially the norepinephrine levels—are either very low or depleted. Low levels of norepinephrine can cause depression, and stress can cause pain, depression, anxiety, uncertainty, and fear.

A person who is depressed may become more depressed when he is alone or in a particular situation which gives rise to distraction. He has no happiness in his life, and there is a feeling of hopelessness and helplessness as to what the future holds. He has no energy. He has no interests. Often he will reach for a drink or drug.

Most alcoholics are depressed. Changes of appetite are quite normal, either to one extreme or the other—i.e., undereating or overeating. Depression exhibits many faces. It constitutes a wide spectrum from sadness or the "blues" that everyone experiences at one time or another through reactive depression caused by the loss of someone or something loved. It extends to psychotic depression in which contact with reality is lost, and there may even be thoughts of suicide or—the ultimate loss—the actual act of suicide. Psychotic depression may or may not be endogenous (i.e., self-produced) depression. It can actually be diet induced. Depression is one of the most common disorders of the mind. Often it is treated with antidepressants and/or tranquilizers.

The affective disorders are divided into two types: unipolar and bipolar. Unipolar is characterized by depression or mania alone. Bipolar is depicted by both depression and mania. The difference is important, for the origin is probably different; likewise, the two disorders have different pharmacological responses.

The widely accepted hypothesis for affective disorders is the catecholamine hypothesis. Although is has various forms, the simplest is that the depression is caused by a metabolism. More evidence is available for the depression than the mania to support the theory. In traditional medicine, the depression is treated with monoamine oxidase inhibitors (MAO's); the inhibitors are believed to exercise their effects by inhibiting the breakdown of norepinephrine.

Another drug used to treat depression is the tricyclic which prevents the re-uptake of the norepinephrine, dopamine, and serotonin from the synaptic cleft. Still another medication used in this treatment is the psychostimulants such as amphetamine and methylphenidate. These drugs work by increasing the amount of norepinephrine available at the synaptic cleft. The increased norepinephrine is via increased release from the storage vesicles, inhibiting monoamine re-uptake. To date, a single mechanism does not fit all the facts of the affective disorders and their pharmacological and therapeutic responses. The cause of depression does not appear to be a single entity.

L-phenylalanine had been used to increase the level of norepinephrine in the brain. The neurotransmitters, especially norepinephrine, are responsible for an elevation and positive moods, alertness and ambition in a person.

Sometimes the norepinephrine level is artificially elevated by drugs such as antidepressants; these drugs work by blocking the norepinephrine from reentering the pouches within the neuron. This blocking causes the artificial manipulation which leads to an elevation of the mood. In actuality, this aggravates the original problem. The natural way to normalize the brain and nerve level of norepinephrine is by providing adequate levels in the diet in the form of L-phenylalanine or L-tyrosine or with supplementation of these amino acids.

DLPA And Depression

Most people think of their emotions as separate from their bodies and unconnected with the chemistry of their brain cells. However, depression, irritability, and anxiety are all reflections of the functioning of the brain. When certain nutrients are not supplied to the brain, it experiences an array of negative emotions, tending to lose its coping ability in response to the stressful circumstances we confront each day of our lives.

Although the brain is only equal to two percent of our total body weight, 25% of our total metabolic activity takes place there. This is probably the reason that the brain is so sensitive to nutritional deficiency. In fact, our need for proper brain function is so great that the body feeds the brain preferentially. Yet, the brain is the most undernourished organ in the body.

Nutrients can cause important changes in the chemical composition of substances in the brain, with corresponding changes in our feelings. Scientific studies show that by taking particular amino acids, mental depression, apathy, peevishness, and the desire to be left alone can be alleviated.

About one in five Americans has significant symptoms of depression, more than 2.5 million are being treated for it, and about 50 million can expect to suffer from it at some point in their lives. Classic, full-blown depression has been described as "the loss of the capacity to enjoy life combined with decreased thought and movement." It can appear as grief, but may manifest itself through a series of emotional states so extreme that the outcome is suicide or total withdrawal.

Of course a preoccupation with death or suicide is an obvious symptom, but often depression is not obvious because the person does not feel "sad." This is called "masked depression." Symptoms may involve changes in sleeping patterns, such as insomnia, early morning waking, constant sleepiness, or changes in eating patterns— either overeating or loss of appetite. The person may be anxious or have excessive complaints about body functions and chronic pain, especially headaches, but also indigestion or constipation. Both hair and skin may feel dry and lack luster, while blood pressure has a tendency to be high. There is an inability to enjoy customary pleasures and a concomitant loss of sex drive, loss of energy, extreme atigue, difficulty concentrating and making decisions, irritability, and possibly temperamental outbursts.

With endogenous depression, there are symptoms of guilt, self-hate, feelings of worthlessness, apathy, crying spells, and a desire to be left alone. Women are more susceptible to depression than men— 1 woman in 6, compared to 1 man in 12. It is thought that there may be some connection to the female reproductive hormone cycles. There are also some diseases, such as hypothyroidism (underactive thyroid gland), that may produce depression, while others, such as arthritis or heart disease, commonly bring on a depressive reaction. Overall, not only can depression be a result of nutritional deficiency, but that depression in turn puts a further stress on the body. Without the proper nutritional attention, depression has a very deleterious effect on the general health.

Treatment

DLPA (or DL-phenylalanine) has been found to be effective in the treatment of depression. Studies since 1974 show it to be particularly beneficial in cases of endogenous depression. This is the type of depression that is characterized by a decrease in energy and interest, feelings of worthlessness, and a pervasive sense of helplessness to control the course of one's life. Significant improvement has also been achieved with people suffering from reactive depression (thought to be caused by environmental influences such as a death in the family) and involutional depression (an aging-related depression). DLPA has also shown itself to be effective for other types of depression, including the depressive phase of manic-depression, schizophrenic depression, and post-amphetamine depression.

Phenylalanine is one of the "essential" amino acids, and it must be obtained through the diet. The type of phenylalanine our bodies require is L-phenylalanine, while the type found to be most effective against depression is D-phenylalanine. D-phenylalanine mirrors L-phenylalanine in its molecular structure. DLPA or the DL-form is the preferable form for depression. DLPA is a 50/50 mixture of D-phenylalanine and L-phenylalanine. They do not interact but follow separate transport and metabolic pathways. In other words, 500 mg of DLPA behaves like 250 mg of pure D-phenylalanine plus 250 mg of L-phenylalanine.

At this time, it appears that DLPA has three separate antidepressant effects in the body: increased production of PEA, increased endorphin levels, and increased norepinephrine production. These biochemical changes are not isolated but rather create a synergistic overlap which accounts for the terrific result of DLPA in the treatment of depression.

Although D-phenylalanine is very rare in nature, all mammals, including man, are able to metabolize it. Part of the metabolic process involves conversion to phenylethylamine or PEA. PEA is a neurotransmitter-type substance which bears a close structural resemblance to the stimulant drug amphetamine. It seems to be a natural stimulant. This characteristic prompted mental health researchers to speculate that a deficiency of PEA in the nervous system might be a cause of depression. This concept gained support when research demonstrated that depressed patients were not just low in PEA, they were "immeasurably low."

In a series of studies in the late 70's, it was also found that every major treatment for depression indirectly elevated levels of PEA in the brain. Both D- and L- forms of phenylalanine are directly converted to PEA. However, D-phenylalanine has been reported to induce greater, more prolonged increases than L-phenylalanine alone. A second way in which DLPA may act as an anti-depressant is in its ability to inhibit enzymes which break down the endorphin hormone. Endorphins are morphine-like hormones whose presence may account for the euphoria experienced by runners, joggers, and other enthusiasts of aerobic exercise. It is thought that endorphin concentration in the brain may be critical in mood regulation. If a sufficient number of the receptors in the brain are filled with endorphins and enkephalins, a person feels a sense of well-being. But, if for some reason the endorphin level is reduced and too few receptors are filled, the deficiency causes a person to feel a sense of urgency and irritation. In a similar way if the production is too high and an excessive number of receptors are filled, a person feels a sense of euphoria that is usually followed by a letdown. This is natural, and is a major cause of the "ups and downs" everyone experiences in life.

If a drug such as heroin or morphine is consumed, these drugs take the place of endorphins and enkephalins at the receptors and, if taken in quantity, activate a large number of receptors, creating an unnatural euphoria. A person feels great for a while, but the drug has a serious side effect. It causes the body to shut down the production of natural endorphins and enkephalins. Then, as the drug wears off, the feeling of need becomes greater than ever. If drug consumption continues over a period of time, the ability of the body to produce endorphins and enkephalins is reduced, and the person becomes dependent on the drug.

A patient who has been taking narcotics or drugs for awhile has desensitized his endorphin receptors. Even if he desired to quit using the narcotics, his body would not respond to an endorphin release. He must gradually reduce his intake of drugs to slowly reactivate his endorphin receptor sites.

In fact, clinical research has shown that endorphins administered intravenously can trigger sudden, dramatic anti-depressant actions, even in suicidal patients. Essentially, DLPA works because it inhibits endorphin-degrading enzymes so that the endorphins produced by the brain last longer.

You will recall that alcohol has been found to cause the production of chemicals called tetrahydroisoquinolines, or TIQ's, which have effects similar to morphine or heroin. They fill the enkephalin receptors, produce an unnatural euphoria, and reduce the output of the natural endorphins and enkephalins. The long term use of large amounts of alcohol produces a permanent urgent need for alcohol, and the craving for more alcohol or another drink.

Additionally, DLPA could be converted to the brain neurotransmitter norepinephrine. A deficiency of norepinephrine was the first brain chemical deficiency believed to be involved in severe depression. Like PEA, norepinephrine is a natural stimulant. Both D- and L-phenylalanine serve as its precursors, although they follow somewhat different metabolic pathways. Most antidepressant drugs are designed to increase the amount of norepinephrine in the central nervous system, but by very different means than DLPA.

Antidepressant drugs, such as tricyclics, can be effective in reducing symptoms of depression. Unfortunately, this is where their usefulness ends. They can engender numerous adverse side effects such as seizures, drowsiness, nausea, and anorexia. They can also stimulate neurotransmitter release for mood elevation, but they prevent reabsorption of the neurotransmitters into nerve terminals. This depletes our cellular stores of neurotransmitter material and interferes with proper brain function. DLPA can serve to restore brain levels to normal.

In a recent double-blind controlled study, DLPA was found to be equally as effective as the tricyclic drug Imipramine, the most commonly prescribed antidepressant. Psychopathological, neurologic, and somatic indices showed no differences between the two treatments. Side effects tended to be higher for the Imipramine patients.

- DL-phenylalanine and Imipramine were given to depressed patients in equal dosages (150-200 mg/day) with 20 patients in each group.
- Psychopathological, neurologic, and somatic indices showed no differences between the two treatments.
- Automatic side effects "tended to be higher for the Imipramine patients."

- Antidepressant efficacy of DL-phenylalanine "seems to equal that of the tricyclic antidepressant Imipramine."

Evidence indicates that DLPA may be useful in alleviating the mood disorders associated with PMS premenstrual syndrome. Reports from clinical investigations have revealed that over 80% of all patients suffering from PMS have experienced good to complete relief.

DLPA dosage comes in capsules of 375 to 750 mg. The dosage is generally 4 to 8 capsules per day. Each capsule should be taken 30 minutes prior to meals. It is important that the capsules be taken in divided dosages throughout the day to get the antidepressant effect. Dosage can be varied with improvement, but must be individualized. People who suffer from PKU (phenylketonuria) should not use DLPA.

Key Factors Of DLPA

1) DLPA is a highly safe, nontoxic substance when used in short- or long-term therapy.

2) DLPA does not induce excessive excitation or arousal in normal or depressed subjects.

3) Toxic overdose is impossible and there is generally a lack of potential for abuse.

4) DLPA does not cause adverse side effects.

Endogenous depression, which was discussed earlier in relation to DLPA, is a particularly insidious mental state. The person involved feels so worthless that they do not want to take the necessary steps to feel good. When a person feels depressed, they do not feel like taking good care of themselves. Of course, that is the very time a person needs to do right—eat right, sleep right, think right, and . . . get enough exercise and amino acids.

L-Tyrosine

Recent clinical findings that the natural amino acid L-tyrosine is helpful in overcoming depression, improving memory, and increasing mental alertness, has stimulated interest in the nutritional role of this dietary factor. Of particular interest is the research linking L-tyrosine deficiency to the development of depression in some oral contraceptive users.

The body needs L-tyrosine to build many complex structural proteins and enzymes. But recent clinical research has centered on the simpler compounds used by the body to transmit nerve impulses which determine a person's mental mood and alertness. These compounds are called neurotransmitters, and they are readily formed in the body by minor alteration of the L-tyrosine molecule. It is very likely that deficiencies of L-tyrosine can impair the body's ability to produce the proper balance of these neurotransmitters.

In assessing the dietary quantity of L-tyrosine, the L-phenylalanine content of the diet should also be determined, as the body can make L-tyrosine out of "left- over" L-phenylalanine. Dietary L-tyrosine can spare the body some (but not all) of its L-phenylalanine need. The best food sources of L-tyrosine are meats, eggs, and dairy products. Clinical researchers prefer to use L-tyrosine supplements rather than rely on whole foods because it is difficult to obtain such amounts in normal diets.

L-tyrosine (or its precursor, L-phenylalanine) is used by the body to produce several compounds which are important to nerve transmission. The adrenal medulla and nerve cells can quickly produce these compounds from L-tyrosine.

Two of these compounds, epinephrine and norepinephrine, have wide ranging activities that affect brain and nerve cells. Both compounds are produced in nerve cells, as well as in the adrenal medulla where they can be stored. A third compound produced from L-tyrosine, dopamine, affects nerve tracts in the brain, in addition to its role in the production of the other two.

These compounds are called neurotransmitters because they control the basic process of impulse transmission between nerve cells. Epinephrine is secreted at nerve terminals in the hypothalamus. Norepinephrine is released at sympathetic nerve (fight-or-flight response) endings, and thus affects the immediate postsynaptic cells. Dopamine transmission appears to be defective in Parkinson's disease.

These neurotransmitters are responsible for an elevated and positive mood, alertness, and ambition. Medical researchers in the past have relied on increasing the brain and nerve levels of norepinephrine by using drugs, such as phenylpropanolamine and amphetamines, which cause the release of norepinephrine, block its return to storage, or slow the destruction of L-tyrosine. However, such artificial manipulation often leads to depletion of the neurotransmitter and the aggravation of the original problem. The natural solution is to normalize brain and nerve levels of norepinephrine by providing adequate levels of dietary L-tyrosine.

Clinical studies have shown that L-tyrosine controls medication-resistant depression. Two studies published in 1980 are of interest. The first was published in the *American Journal of Psychiatry* by Dr. Alan J. Gelenberg of the Department of Psychiatry at Harvard

Medical School. Dr. Gelenberg discussed the role of L-tyrosine in controlling anxiety and depression. He postulated that a lack of available L-tyrosine results in a deficiency of the hormone norepinephrine at a specific brain location, which, in turn, relates to mood problems such as depression.

Dr. Gelenberg treated patients having long-standing depression not responding to standard therapy by administering dietary supplements of L-tyrosine. Within two weeks of daily intakes of 1,000 milligrams per day of a L-tyrosine supplement tremendous improvement was noted. Patients were able to discontinue or reduce amphetamines to minimal levels in a matter of weeks.

The second study was published in *Lancet* by Dr. I. Goldberg. Allergy sufferers have also responded well to L-tyrosine supplementation, as well as those on weight loss programs. Pearson reports that L-tyrosine supplementation is a preferred way to control appetite, rather than phenylpropanolamine or amphetamine administration which causes norepinephrine release only.

Cocaine addiction has been helped with daily supplementation of doses of at least 3000 mg per day in divided dosages. Additionally, GABA in doses of 3000 mg per day has reduced the stress and anxiety associated with cocaine addiction. Other important amino acids and nutrients include DLPA—2000 mg per day, Siberian ginseng—1000-1500 mg per day, glutamine 2000 mg per day.

Tyrosine Or DLPA Cannot Be Taken With The Following Medications
Caution: These Drugs Are Addictive.

Brand Name/ Generic Name	Half-life	Toxic Side Effects
Tofranil (Imipramine)	11 - 24 hrs.	Sedation, weight gain, dizziness
Pamelor, Aventyl (Nortriptyline)	18 - 44 hrs.	Zonked feeling, mental dysfunction, lethargy
Aventyl (Nortriptyline)	18 - 44 hrs.	Fatigue, mental dullness, sedated
Elavil (Amitriptyline)	31 - 46 hrs.	Dry mouth, constipation, blurred vision
Norpramin (Desipramine)	12 - 24 hrs.	Shakiness, problem sleeping, blurred vision

Tyrosine Or DLPA Cannot Be Taken With The Following Medications
Caution: These Drugs Are Addictive.

Brand Name/ Generic Name	Half-life	Toxic Side Effect(s)
Sinequan (Doxepin)	8 - 24 hrs.	Constipation, nervous restlessness
Vivactil (Protriptyline)	67 - 89 hrs.	Confusion, weakness, irregular heartbeat
Wellbutrin (Bupropion)	8 - 24 hrs.	Agitation, anxiety, confusion
Desyrel (Trazodone)	3 - 9 hrs.	Blurred vision, fatigue, anger
Effexor (Venlafaxine)	16 hrs.	Insomnia, dry mouth, anxiety

These drugs must be used with caution. Once you begin using them you should not discontinue abruptly. Consult a health care professional for assistance.

L-Tryptophan

Tryptophan is an essential amino acid which is the precursor of serotonin. Serotonin is synthesized from tryptophan. Serotonin is a brain neurotransmitter, platelet clotting factor, and neurohormone found in the organs throughout the body. Tryptophan is essential to maintain the body's protein balance. When food that is protein deficient or lacking tryptophan is fed to growing or mature individuals, such foods fail to replace worn-out materials which are lost by the body during the organic activities of its cells, tissues, and organs. The amino acid tryptophan is used up in the vital activities of the body, and in turn, must be replaced to prevent atrophy of the body's structures.

Tryptophan is one of the few substances capable of passing the blood-brain barrier. It has a variety of important roles in mental activity. When tryptophan intake is deficient, especially during periods of stress, serotonin levels drop, yielding depression, anxiety, insecurity, hyperactivity, insomnia, and pain. To have enough tryptophan, the body must have an ample supply of Vitamin B6, without which tryptophan cannot be formed.

Tryptophan's role in behavior has been demonstrated by the number of mental functions that it directly influences. Serotonin produces a relaxed, calm, secure, mellow, and morphine-like analgesic feeling. Hyperactive children/adults have a low serotonin level. Supplements containing tryptophan and Vitamin B6 can correct some of the biochemical disorders related to aggression.

Another significant finding in studies done with tryptophan demonstrated that low levels of serotonin could play a part in the development of depression. When tryptophan (1,000 mg) at bedtime is combined with tyrosine in doses of 3,000 mg per day, they can mimic the effects of most antidepressants. Tryptophan is useful in unipolar depression or constant, low-grade depression with no highs or lows.

Both depression and pain can have a profound effect on the ability of a person to fall asleep. Difficulty in falling asleep can be caused by low serotonin levels. But tryptophan has been shown to be very effective in insomnia problems, reducing the time needed to fall asleep and increasing the number of hours spent sleeping. The usual dosage is 500 to 1,000 mg taken one hour prior to bedtime with a carbohydrate such as orange juice or fruit.

Tryptophan is only available by prescription. For information call The Medicine Shoppe at 1-800-542-5767.

Because serotonin is a neurotransmitter, it is one of the most important chemicals that helps control moods as well. Best of all, tryptophan is safe and is a natural relaxant and tranquilizer of the central nervous system. The body has no difficulty in rapidly metabolizing and clearing it from the body. It is an essential amino acid which is necessary for life, and is the sole precursor for serotonin. It does not simply pass through the gut into the brain to become serotonin. It must compete with five other amino acids—tyrosine, phenylalanine, leucine, isoleucine, and valine—at the blood brain barrier. In order to increase the amount of brain serotonin, the ratio of tryptophan must be elevated out of proportion to the competing amino acids. Metabolism and protein intake may alter this ratio.

About 90 percent of serum tryptophan is bound to albumin. Free fatty acids (serum) share the same albumin binding sites. Changing both the blood sugar level and insulin may increase and decrease the proportion of free tryptophan that has access to the brain. In the total serum amino acid profile the ratio of tryptophan to the nutrient amino acids has been elevated in each instance. Tyrosine has also been elevated in each instance. About 1 percent of the ingested tryptophan is metabolized to serotonin. About 90 percent of the tryptophan is metabolized through kynurenic acid to nicotinic acid.

The neurotransmitters are directly dependent on dietary tryptophan and other amino acids. It has been found that there are circadian rhythms that are associated with the amino acid utilization in the nervous system. Circadian rhythm is a specific type of periodicity for the uptake and utilization of substances. This has recently been shown with regard to the use of tryptophan in the treatment of insomnia. When tryptophan is used during the day it does not seem to induce sleep, only a calm relaxed state; but when taken near bedtime it seems to induce sleep, as shown in sleep studies done at several medical centers. This seems to indicate that tryptophan's uptake across the blood-brain barrier is tied to the circadian rhythms of the sleep cycle. Its absorption is facilitated in the brain in its conversion to serotonin more effectively during times when a person would normally sleep. This is why it is clinically suggested to administer tryptophan at bedtime if it is to be used for treating sleep disorders. Conversely, tryptophan or tyrosine should be used during the day to treat certain forms of depression. Aggression is one of the most widely recognized signs of reduced serotonin. Liquid serotonin used 3 to 4 times daily will elevate the serotonin level. Melatonin also elevates the serotonin level and is effective for sleep problems. Melatonin is produced by the pineal gland in the brain. Melatonin is a neurohormone.

Two researchers in England compared the antidepressant effects of tryptophan and Tofranil. (Tofranil is a drug which is commonly used for depression.) Both groups of patients with depression improved. The conclusion of their study revealed tryptophan was just as effective as the laboratory-produced drug, and there were no side effects from the tryptophan. Conversely, the side effects for the Tofranil group included blurring of the vision, dryness of the mouth, low blood pressure, urinary retention, heart palpitations, hepatitis, and seizures.

L-tryptophan is obtained in the diet everyday. Many rich natural forms of tryptophan include: bananas, green leafy vegetables, red meat, milk, pineapple, avocados, and eggs. Large doses of tryptophan when combined with niacinamide and vitamin B6 can enhance the conversion of tryptophan to serotonin.

Amino acids have an impact on brain neurochemistry; they actually influence neuro-regulatory substances that may ultimately clinically cause changes in mind, mood, memory, and behavior.

L-Cysteine

Research is focusing on the protective role of dietary amino acids. L-cysteine is of interest, not only because it builds proteins such as those in hair, but because it helps destroy harmful chemicals in the body such as acetaldehyde and free radicals produced by smoking and drinking. The natural form of cystine found in foods is designated L-cysteine.

L-cysteine is the stable form of the sulfur-containing amino acid cysteine. Both forms are amino acids, and the body readily interconverts one into the other as needed. Thus, the two forms may be considered as a single amino acid in metabolism.

Cysteine is more soluble in water than L-cystine, but both are very soluble in acid solutions. However, solubility should not be confused with digestibility or assimilation.

L-cysteine spares methionine (another important amino acid) and can completely replace dietary methionine if the diet is supplemented by appropriate amounts of folic acid and vitamin B12.

L-cysteine is abundant in proteins such as keratin in hair (12%) and trypsinogen (10%). L-cysteine has been used as a food supplement and as a detoxicant. Heavy metals such as mercury, lead and cadmium will be "tied up" by either the sulfur released by L-cysteine or by the sulfhydryl group in L-cysteine.

Heavy drinkers and smokers may be protected by L-cysteine against acetaldehyde poisoning from chronic alcohol intake or smoking, according to Dr. Herbert Sprince and his associates at the Veterans Administration Hospital, Coatesville, Pennsylvania, and Thomas Jefferson University, Philadelphia, Pennsylvania.

Pearson reports that this amino acid is effective "not only in preventing hangovers, but also in preventing brain and liver damage from alcohol, and in preventing damage such as emphysema and cancer caused by smoking."

L-cysteine has been found to offer a degree of protection against radiation.

Recently, Dr. William Philpott has postulated that L-cysteine is necessary for the utilization of vitamin B-6. His studies suggest that "a majority of chronic degenerative illnesses, whether physical or mental, have a vitamin B-6 utilization disorder. The culprit in this vitamin B-6 utilization problem seems to be L-cysteine deficiency." Dr. Philpott recommends patients having the vitamin B-6 utilization problem take 1.5 grams of L-cysteine three times a day for a month and then reduce it to twice a day.

L-Carnitine

Recent research indicates that L-carnitine plays an important role in converting stored body fat into energy, controlling hypoglycemia, energizing the heart, reducing angina attacks, and is beneficial to patients having diabetes, liver disease, or kidney disease.

L-carnitine helps to transport long-chain fatty acids. By

preventing fatty build up, this unique amino acid aids the body by decreasing the risk for heart disease, weight loss, increased energy and even works to decrease pain. L-carnitine can be manufactured in the body if L-lysine and B vitamins are available. L-carnitine is an excellent nutrient to add to your daily program, especially if you have a problem with elevated cholesterol.

L-carnitine deficient people often have severe bouts of hypoglycemia. The sugar addict and the alcoholic have been known to have problems with hypoglycemia. When the blood sugar drops, the person may reach for a drink to rapidly increase his blood sugar; hypoglycemia is one of the multitude of theories about the causes of alcoholism and addiction.

L-carnitine plays an important role in the production of heat in "brown fat." "Brown fat" is the fat tissue that helps us acclimate to cold temperatures, and is thought to help determine how much of the food we eat is burned for heat and how much is converted into stored body-fat. L-carnitine also prevents ketones from accumulating to cause "acid blood" during poor weight-loss diets. This condition is called *ketosis*, and when uncontrolled can be life-threatening. Even when not life-threatening, ketosis causes the loss of important minerals such as potassium, calcium, and magnesium.

Dietary Sources of L-Carnitine

The major sources of dietary L-carnitine are meat and dairy products. Vegetables, fruits, and cereals contain little or no L-carnitine. All milks are rich in L-carnitine, and several studies suggest that L-carnitine is an essential nutrient for the newborn.

Heart Disease

The heart produces most of its energy from fats, and thus is dependent upon L-carnitine. An L-carnitine deficiency causes extreme metabolic impairment to heart tissue. On the other hand, supplemental L-carnitine has proved to be beneficial to heart patients. L-carnitine (20 or 40 mg/kg body weight) has increased the endurance of heart patients for exercise. Other studies have shown that L-carnitine (40 mg/kg body weight) lowers the exercise heart rate, extends the time of exercise prior to the onset of angina, and at 100 mg/kg body weight, reduces the number of angina attacks and nitroglycerine consumption.

Cirrhosis and Carnitine

Cirrhosis is a disease in which fibrous tissue displaces healthy liver tissue and liver functions are compromised. One of these functions happens to be the last step in the biochemical synthesis of carnitine, and people with cirrhosis show significant reductions in blood carnitine.

Taurine

The biological significance of taurine is now recognized by a growing number of nutritional and neurological researchers. There is strong evidence suggesting that this important amino acid is an essential dietary compound for humans and that deprivation of the newborn of a dietary source of taurine may have deleterious results. Taurine is needed for normal development and health of the central nervous system. Disturbances in taurine metabolism are seen in problems as diverse as epilepsy and heart disease.

Taurine is a naturally occurring amino acid that does not occur in proteins. Taurine is found in appreciable concentrations in the brain, and more taurine is found in the brain than in other tissues. Taurine protects and stabilizes the brain's fragile membranes and acts as a neurotransmitter. Only in the last couple of years has taurine been added to the growing list of neurotransmitters. Taurine seems to be closely related in its structure and metabolism to other neurotransmitters such as glycine and GABA. Taurine, like GABA, is inhibitory.

Taurine, or a modified taurine, may someday supersede synthetic tranquilizers. Research is now in progress. Antiseizure activity in epilepsy has been demonstrated with taurine intakes between 200 and 1,500 milligrams per day, although intakes as high as 7,000 milligrams have been used.

Taurine also plays an important part in bile formation, and thus is important to fat metabolism and blood cholesterol control. This could prove very helpful in the alcoholic or sugar addict for fat metabolism and liver function.

In many mammals, taurine is synthesized from L-cysteine. However, in man, the bulk of the taurine is derived from dietary sources or produced from cysteine. An outstanding dietary source of taurine is animal/fish protein and marine animals, especially Mollusca (oysters, clams, mussels, snails).

Amino Acids and Nutrients For Clinical Conditions and Diseases

The following list *is only* a guideline for specific conditions. Each individual's needs are different. Some nutrients will help you more than others. Therefore, you must find the nutrients that best suit your situation.

CONDITION	SUGGESTED THERAPY	AVOID
Aging	Methionine, Tryptophan, Glutamine, BNC + GABA, Melatonin, Ester C, Pyncogenol	
Aggressiveness	Tryptophan, GABA, Glycine, Glutamine, Taurine, Tyrosine, B6 Liquid Serotonin, BNC + GABA	Phenylalanine
Alzheimer's	BNC + GABA, Glutamine, Ginkgo B6 (Timed Release), DMG, Pynocogenol	
Arthritis	Histidine, Cysteine, BNC + GABA, Boswella, Malic Acid +, DLPA, Ester C, Magnesium, Niacinamide, Shark Cartilage	
Autism	Tryptophan, Glutamine, B6, Taurine, Liquid Serotonin, Magnesium	
Body Building	BCAA, Alanine, Carnitine	
Cancer	Cysteine, Taurine, Glutamine BNC+ GABA, Ester C, Shark Cartilage, BCAA, Melatonin, Pycnogenol	With Melanoma Phenylalanine, Tyrosine
Cholesterol	Carnitine, Methionine, Arginine Glycine, Taurine, Fortified Flax, Chromium Picolinate	
Chronic Illness	BCAA, BNC + GABA, Cystine, Tryptophan, Ester C, Pycnogenol	
Chronic Pain	Tryptophan, DLPA, GABA, Glutamine, BNC + GABA, Boswella, Ester C, Magnesium	
Cirrhosis / G.I Healing	Glutamine, Carnitine, BCAA, CoEnzyme Q10,	
Depression	Tryptophan, Phenylalanine, Tyrosine, Methionine, GABA Carnitine, Threonine, Taurine	Arginine
Diabetes	Alanine, Cysteine, Tryptophan Carnitine, Magnesium, Chromium Picolinate, Pyconogenol, Ester C	
Drug Addiction	GABA, Methionine, Tyrosine Glutamine, DLPA, B Complex Tryptophan, B6 (Timed Release)	Alcohol

Energy	Carnitine, Tyrosine, CoEnzyme Q10	
Epilepsy	Glycine, Taurine, GABA, B6, Melatonin	
Gallbladder	Methionine, Taurine, Glycine BCAA	
Gout	Glycine	
Hair Loss	Cysteine, Arginine	
Heart Failure	Taurine, Tyrosine, Carnitine, BCAA CoEnzyme Q10, Magnesium	
Herpes	Lysine, Ester C	
Hyperactivity	GABA, Glycine, Glutamine, Taurine, Liquid Serotonin, Tryptophan, BNC + GABA	
Hypertension	Tryptophan, GABA, Taurine, Tyrosine with meals, Magnesium, Calcium, CoEnzyme Q 10	
Hypoglycemia	Alanine, GABA, Chromium Picolinate, Vanadium, Magnesium	
Insomnia	Tryptophan, Melatonin, Liquid Serotonin, GABA	Phenylalanine
Kidney Failure	BNC + GABA, Carnitine,	
Leg Ulcers	Topical Cysteine, Glycine, Threonine, BCAA, Ester C, Zinc	
Liver Disease	BCAA, Carnitine, Glutamine, B6	
Manic	Tryptophan, GABA, Glycine, BNC + GABA, Glutamine	Phenylalanine
Memory Concentration	Glutamine, GABA, Ginkgo BNC + GABA, B6 (Timed Release),	
Mental Alertness	Tyrosine, Phenylalanine, Glutamine, Ginkgo	
Parkinson's	Phenylalanine, Tyrosine, Tryptophan, Methionine, Magnesium, Ester C	
Radiation	Cysteine, Glutamine, Taurine Ester C, Beta Carotene, Pycogenol	
Schizophrenia	GABA, Isoleucine, Tryptophan Methionine, B6, NonFlush Niacin	Serine, Leucine Aspargine
Seizures /Tics	Taurine, GABA,	
Stress	Tyrosine, GABA, Histidine, BNC + GABA, Glutamine, B6, Glycine, Ester C, Magnesium	

Surgery	BCAA, BNC + GABA, Glutamine, Ester C, Beta Carotene
Tardive Dyskinesia	GABA, Taurine, BCAA Glutamine
Tobacco Addiction	Tyrosine, GABA, Tryptophan Glutamine, Methionine, B Complex
Weight Control	Tryptophan, Phenylalanine, GABA, Tyrosine, HCA

Amino acids are involved in many metabolic pathways in the body. They are extremely important as detoxifying and immune stimulating agents. Detoxifying amino acids include cyteine, glutamine, glycine, methionine, taurine and tyrosine. Immunostimulating amino acids include: alanine, aspartic acid, cysteine, glycine, lysine and threonine.

Drug-Nutrient Actions

Drug/ Condition	Parallel Nutrient	Opposite Nutrient
Anticonvulsants	Taurine, GABA, Glycine, Tryptophan, Magnesium	Aspartic Acid
Antidepressants	Phenylalanine, Tyrosine, Methionine, Taurine	Glycine, Histidine
Heart Failure	Taurine, CoEnzyme Q10, Carnitine, Magnesium	Niacin, Tryptophan
Cholesterol / Triglyceride Reducers	Carnitine, Chromium Picolinate	
Steroids (anabolic)	BCAA, Carnitine	Glutamic Acid,
Viral antagonists	Lysine, Zinc	Arginine

Esterfied C

Vitamin C is most important in the treatment of anxiety, stress, depression, and pain. In 1987, clinical studies established that Ester C Polyascorbate is totally neutral, having a pH of 7.0. It does not cause gastrointestinal upset or diarrhea. It is proven four times more bioavailable than ordinary vitamin C.

Esterfied C is a unique complex mixture with a distinctive molecular personality. This means that this form of vitamin C is most available to the tissues of the body, and is available within 20 minutes after ingestion, and 24 hours later some of it is still there. Ordinary vitamin C is out of the body within 4 hours after ingestion; even time-release vitamin C has been excreted while the esterfied vitamin C is still working and available to the body.

All humans, adults, and children need vitamin C, and they need it daily. Esterfied C has been extremely effective in our detoxification program. At The Pain & Stress Center, we use varying doses for adults in detoxification ranging from 2,000 to 10,000 mg daily.

Melatonin

Melatonin, a neurohormone is produced in a tiny gland at the base of the brain. It is called the pineal gland because it resembles a pine cone, and is about the size of a pea.

In the evening hours the pineal gland reacts to diminishing levels of daylight. It starts producing melatonin which is released into the blood and flows through the body making you drowsy. The secretion of melatonin peaks in the middle of the night during your heaviest hours of sleep. In the morning, bright light shining through the eye reaches the pineal gland which reacts by switching off the production of melatonin, thus, removing the sleep state.

The pineal gland is connected to the rest of the hormonal system, and melatonin production can and does influence the functioning in other parts of the body. During darkness and sleep, melatonin modifies the secretion of hormones from organs such as the pituitary.

The pituitary gland is the master gland of the hormonal system. The pituitary, in turn, regulates the secretion of hormones controlling growth, metabolism, thyroid and the adrenal gland.

Since the duration of daylight changes both daily and seasonally, melatonin effectively tells the cells in the body the time of the year and the day. Melatonin controls the circadian rhythm in the body. The circadian rhythm has a central role in the energy involved in all metabolic processes such as the sleep-wake cycle. Research conducted at Massachusetts Institute of Technology and released in February, 1994 showed small amounts of melatonin can bring on the sleep without the narcotic effect of drugs. For best results, melatonin should be taken an hour or two before bed.

Vitamins And Nutrients That Aid In Recovery From Drugs

Nutrient	Usage	Therapeutic Dosage
Vitamin E	Detoxification, antioxidant	Start with 400 I.U. then increase to 800 I.U. after two weeks and continue daily.
Esterfied C	Detoxification	2,000-5,000 mg /day
B Complex	Important in nervous system. Important cofactor in many body reactions	100 mg twice /day
Mag Link	Mental Function	500-1,000 mg
Beta Carotene	Detoxification, antioxidant	10,000 I.U. daily
Multiple Vitamin	Replenish body	If tablet, break in half, half, take 1/2 in AM and 1/2 in PM.
Anxiety Control 24* OR	Antianxiety formula (complete formula)	1 or 2 three times throughout the day.
GABA 750*	Any anxiety	Dissolved in water 2 to 3 times daily, spread out. Must be pure GABA.
Tyrosine	Depression	850-1,000 mg 2 to 3 times daily, spread out
Ginseng	Adaptagen. Increases body's resistance	500-1,000 mg daily AM & PM for stress.
Brain Link	Hyperactivity / A.D.D.	1 scoop 3 times daily.

* Do not take these two together.

Amino Acids And Nutrients That Can Be Used For Recovery From Substance Abuse Dependency On a Daily Basis

Nutrient	Amount	Therapeutic Action	Behavior Change
L-Tyrosine	2,000-3,000 mg spread throughout day	Increases norepinephrine, dopamine	Antianxiety, Antistress, Antidepressant
Tryptophan (Prescription only)	2,000 mg AM & PM	Precursor loading Decreases pain and depression	Anticraving Reduces Insomnia
Glutamine	3,000 mg (1,000 mg 3 times per day)	Precursor loading	Anticraving Antistress
P 5 P (Pyridoxal-5-Phosphate)	10-20 mg	Promotes absorption of amino acids	Facilitates neurotransmitters
B Complex	100 mg	Assists action of amino acids	
GABA	3,000 mg/daily spread throughout day. Use as free-form.	Fills GABA receptors	Antianxiety
Esterfied C	3,000-5,000 mg spread throughout day.	Facilitates action of nutrients and amino acids	Antioxidant Antitoxin
Multi-Vitamin (Good)	1 daily	Provides minimum daily requirement	
DLPA 750	2 daily	Helps keep endorphin level and mood up. Helpful with chronic pain	Mood elevation Pain relief
Ginkgo Biloba	120 mg daily	Enhances memory after drug use	
B A M	2 daily	Provides essential amino acids in balanced formula	
Brain Link	3 times daily	To fuel multi-vitamin, B vitamins and amino acid requirements.	

Trends in Substance Abuse

Alcohol

More than nine million people are believed to have a definite problem with alcohol. The past fifteen years have shown a 30 percent increase in alcohol consumption.

Tobacco

Tobacco is second to alcohol in its widespread use. Fifty-five million Americans smoke cigarettes daily. It is estimated that more than 300,000 people die prematurely each year from illnesses related to smoking. Currently, about 22 percent of youths and 40 percent of adults are regular smokers.

Marijuana

Cannabis is the most commonly used illegal drug. The rates are highest among the 18 to 25 year olds, but its use is spreading to those younger and older. Ten percent of high school seniors are daily users. The most common adverse reaction to marijuana is a state of acute anxiety, sometimes accompanied by paranoid thoughts.

Heroin

The number of those addicted to heroin has stabilized during the past few years at about a half million people. Heroin potency in street material is down to 5 percent, and the cost per pure milligram of heroin has risen to about two dollars. The increased price and decreased potency are believed to reflect a diminished availability.

Methadone

Methadone has become a drug of abuse through its use as a maintenance treatment for about 80,000 users. Since it is effective for about 24 to 36 hours during maintenance therapy, take-home supplies are given to those patients who are allowed to visit the clinic only two or three times a week.

Barbiturates

The source of black market barbiturates and other hypnotics is usually from prescription drugs but they are supplemented with illegitimately manufactured products.

Minor Tranquilizers

In 1987, ninety million prescriptions for minor tranquilizers were filled; there was a slight decrease from the previous year. One fourth of all drug-related emergency room visits are connected with tranquilizer usage.

Amphetamines

Amphetamines and other appetite-suppressant prescription drugs accounted for almost seventeen million prescriptions in 1987.

Reports available show they were used for narcolepsy, minimal brain dysfunction, and (in short courses) weight control. The level of abuse is holding steady. Amphetamines remain a potential item of increased abuse.

Cocaine

Cocaine use continues to increase, with most of those who indulge doing so sporadically. This pattern may be due to its high cost and relative availability. The abuse of this drug is expected to increase during the next few years.

LSD and Other Hallucinogens

LSD, DMT, and other hallucinogenic drugs have declined in use since the mid 1960's, but they have by no means disappeared from the drug scene. Use of PCP or "angel-dust" is on the increase; the results of its ingestion concerns health care professionals and law enforcement officials. The person under the influence of PCP is more apt to engage in unpredictable, violent behavior than has been encountered with other hallucinogens. The individual may present a variety of neurologic and psychiatric toxic reactions that are not easily diagnosed nor treated.

Inhalants

The sniffing of commercial products containing solvents or the contents of aerosol sprays is a juvenile practice that does not always terminate when one becomes an adult. The practice is on the increase. Sudden sniffing death and chronic organ damage have been documented with the use of aerosol sprays. Drug dependence should be viewed as a persistent beginning from a low degree of dependence seen in social or experimental usage to physical dependency or addiction. Drug dependence or addiction can be considered from two aspects: one relates to the interaction between the drug and the individual; the other to the interaction between the drug abuse and society—environmental, sociological, and economic. Investigation of drug abuse is currently proceeding along these two areas as well as the interaction of the two aspects.

In conclusion, two questions must be answered:
1. What brain chemicals are possibly in excess or deficit in the potential addict?
2. What biological markers exist that can help in predicting high-risk groups or individuals?

Consensus in research matters reveals that certain mental states such as depression and schizophrenia are caused in part by a deficit of norepinephrine and an excess of dopamine, respectively.

Additionally, there are theories describing deficits of brain internal opiates called endorphins occurring in compulsive diseases such as alcohol and drug-seeking behavior.

Prozac, Zoloft & Paxil are all classified as antidepressants. These drugs are called selective serotonin reuptake inhibitors or SSRI's. Serotonin is a major neurotransmitter, a chemical messenger in the brain. Serotonin is the most widespread neurotransmitter in the brain. When your serotonin level is low your behavior reflects it. Aggression is one of the most widely recognized symptoms of reduced serotonin. Prozac, Zoloft and Paxil blocks or inhibits the reuptake process for serotonin. This process increases the amount of serotonin in the are of the brain that directly effects behavior. By blocking the uptake of serotonin neuron activity there are more neurotransmitters available to make you feel better. This process is chemically engineered and therefore your behavior and mood are dependent on prescriptions. Stop the prescriptions and the symptoms return. The serotonin level in the brain can be elevated by the amino acid tryptophan without any potential for adverse side effects or dependency. Serotonin comes from tryptophan and melatonin.

Antidepressants are the most common class of drugs to produce serotonin syndrome. Serotonin syndrome involves overstimulating of the brain stem and spinal cord producing symptoms of irrational euphoria, headache, seizures, anxiety, agitation and dizziness. Those drugs that can produce serotonin syndrome are antidepressants, the monamine oxidase inhibitors (MAO, SSRI's, & the tricyclic antidepressants Anafranil and Tofranil). All of these drugs have a potential for addiction and abuse. Tryptophan cannot be taken at the same time as Prozac, Zoloft, or Paxil. You must first detox from the prescription drugs. Do not stop any of these drugs abruptly, follow the detoxification program outlined. Decrease day by 5 mg. per seven days. It takes approximately two weeks to clear all Prozac from your body.

Paxil (brand) ~ Paroxetine (generic)

Major Side Effects: This drug is not to be discontinued suddenly (without physician's guidance), as depression may return quickly and more severely than when the drug was first started. A generalized feeling of weakness*, sweating*, nausea*, dry mouth*, constipation*, or diarrhea, decrease in appetite, drowsiness*, insomnia, shakiness*, nervousness*, anxiety and sexual disturbance* (male more than female).

Interactions With Other Medications: Not to be taken with alcohol. Products or foods containing tryptophan are not recommended and may cause severe headache, nausea, sweating and dizziness. Patients who currently take warfarin (**Coumadin**), cimetadine (**Tagamet**) or digoxin (**Lanoxin**), may need to have the dosages of the drugs adjusted by their physician, after **Paxil** is added to the regimen. Over-the-counter drugs such as decongestants and antihistamines may increase the severity of certain side effects. Patients who are switching from **Prozac, Zoloft** or other antidepressants must do so cautiously, under a physician's guidance, to prevent certain side effects from becoming critical There may be a possibility of an interaction with sumitriptan (**Imitrex**), however available studies have not been able to produce consistent results.

Effexor (brand) ~ Venlafaxine (generic)

Major Side Effects: A general feeling of weakness or tiredness*, sweating*, nausea*, vomiting*, constipation, upset stomach*, anorexia with weight loss*, sleep disturbances*, dry mouth, dizziness*, increase in blood pressure*, anxiety or nervousness*, tremor*, blurred vision, sexual dysfunction*, impotence*, yawning*, chills*.

Interactions With Other Medications: Not to taken with alcohol. Certain drugs used over-the-counter such as antihistamines and decongestants may have and additive effect regarding certain side effects. Cimetadine (**Tagamet HB, Tagamet**) may in some patients (especially with liver disease) cause more of Effexor to enter the blood stream than is normal. Patients taking routine blood pressure medication need to monitor their blood pressure regularly, especially on higher doses of Effexor. Effexor should not be taken with other similar drugs (**Prozac, Paxil, Zoloft**) or any other antidepressant medications, unless recommended by your psychiatrist.

Zoloft (brand) ~ Sertraline (generic)

Major Side Effects: Do not discontinue taking this drug suddenly (without physician's guidance), as depression may return quickly and more severely than when the drug was first started. Dry mouth, increased sweating, dizziness, headache, nausea, diarrhea, upset stomach (eating before taking the drug may help prevent stomach symptoms), sleeplessness, sexual dysfunction (more incidence in males than females) and restlessness.

Interactions With Other Medications: Not to be taken with alcohol. Some side effects become more serious with over-the-counter drugs, such as decongestants and antihistamines. Products containing tryptophan are not recommended, and may cause severe headaches, nausea, sweating and dizziness. Cimetadine (**Tagamet**) may increase the amount of Zoloft in the system, causing an increase in certain side effects. Bleeding times may be increased in patients already taking warfarin (**Caumadin**). Patients switching from

Prozac, **Paxil** or other antidepressants must do so cautiously under a physician's care to prevent certain side effects from becoming critical. There may be a possibility of an interaction with sumitriptan (**Imitrex**), however, available studies have not been able to produce consistent results.

Serzone (brand) ~ Nefazodone (generic)

Major Side Effects: Headache, drowsiness*, dry mouth, nausea*, and upset stomach, dizziness*, Blurred or abnormal vision*, sexual dysfunction, light-headedness, confusion*, constipation*, loss of strength and energy, and postural hypotension (drop in blood pressure when going from a sitting position to a standing position).

Interactions With Other Medications: Not to be taken with alcohol. Serious and possibly fatal reactions could occur while taking monoamine oxidase inhibitors (MAOIs), for example **Nardil** or **Parnate**, with nefazodone. Patients who have stopped taking MAOI must wait at least 2 weeks before starting nefazodone. Patients who have stopped taking serzone must wait 1 week before starting an MAOI. Nefazodone should also not be taken with triazolam (**Halcion**) or alprazolam (**Xanax**), especially in elderly patients, where interaction may cause serious thinking and movement impairment. Terfenadine (**Seldane**), astemizole (**Hismanal**), and cisapride (**Propulsid**) are also not recommended for use with serzone, due to possibility of negative side effects on the heart.

Risperdal (brand) ~ Risperidone (generic)

Major Side Effects: Extrapyramidal effects*, dizziness, agitation, anxiety*, and nervousness, sleep disorders, weight gain, headache, constipation*, upset stomach*, nausea, drowsiness* (which may affect ability to drive), tiredness, sun-sensitivity, and sexual dysfunction.

Interactions With Other Medications: Not to be taken with alcohol. Certain drugs used in the treatment of Parkinson's disease (**Sinemet, Levadopa**) may be rendered less effective when reperidone is added to current drug therapy. Carbamazepine (**Tegretol**) may interfere with resperidone's effectiveness by clearing risperidone from the body too quickly. Clozapine (**Clozaril**), another psychotropic drug, may increase the effect of risperidone by slowing down the rate at which risperidone clears from the body. Certain over-the-counter medications such as antihistamines found in cough and cold remedies may have an additive effect on the severity of some side effects.

Prozac (brand) ~ Fluoxetine (generic)

Major Side Effects: This drug must not be discontinued suddenly (without physician's guidance) as depression may return quickly and more severely than when the drug was first started. Headache, nervousness, sleeplessness, drowsiness, anxiety, shakiness, dizziness, general feeling of weakness or fatigue, nausea and upset stomach (take with food or milk), diarrhea, decreased appetite, constipation, and decrease in sexual desire (male & female). Some side effects may lessen in severity or even subside within a few weeks of therapy.

Interactions With Other Medications: Not to be taken with alcohol. Products or foods containing tryptophan (i.e., poultry, veal, some health store protein powders) are not recommended and may cause severe headache, nausea, sweating and dizziness. Patients currently taking carbamazepine (**Tegretol**), lithium warfarin (**Coumadin**), phenytoin (**Dilantin**) and cimetadine (**Tagamet**) may need to have the dosages of these drugs adjusted by their physician after Prozac is added to the regimen. Over-the-counter drugs such as decongestants and antihistamines may increase the severity of certain side effects. There may be a possibility of an interaction with sumitriptan (**Imitrex**), however, available studies have not been able to produce consistent results. There have been reports that patients taking buspirone (**Buspar**), especially for OCD, have had a worsening of their condition when Prozac was added.

Luvox (brand) ~ Fluvoxamine (generic)

Major Side Effects: Unlike the other SSRI antidepressants, Luvox has a tendency to make patients drowsy, and therefore is recommended to be given at bedtime. Some patients, however, may still experience sleeplessness, nervousness, anxiety, dizziness, shakiness, feeling of general weakness, nausea, vomiting and upset stomach, lack of appetite, sexual dysfunction, dry mouth and sweating. May of these side effects lessen in severity or disappear with continued use of the drug. Do not stop taking this drug suddenly without prescriber's knowledge or consent, as OCD symptoms may return, worse than before the drug therapy.

Interactions With Other Medications: Not to be taken with alcohol. Products or foods containing tryptophan (poultry and powdered protein drink mixes are among the highest) are not recommended, and may cause severe headache, nausea, sweating and dizziness. This same reaction can occur with tramadol (**Ultram**), fenfluramine (**Pondimen "Phen-fen" diet**) and the newer dexfenfluramine (**ReDux**). Over-the-counter drugs containing decongestants or antihistamines may increase the severity of certain side effects, impairing judgement while driving. Dextromethoraphan ("**DM**" in many over-the-counter and prescription cough preparations) and codeine have been documented to cause hallucinations in patients taking SSRIs. Patients who are switching from another antidepressant (such as **Prozac**, **Zoloft**, or **Paxil**) must do so cautiously under a physician's guidance. There may be a possibility of an interaction with sumitriptan (**Imitrex**), however available studies have not been able to produce consistent results. Patients already on drugs such as propanolol (**Inderol**), metoprolol (**Lopressor**), carbamazepine (**Tegretol**), clozapine (**Clozaril**), diltiazem (**Cardizem**), lithium, methadone, theophylline (**Theo-Dur, Slo-BID**) and warfarin (**Coumadin**), may have to make adjustments (usually a decrease) to the usual doses of these drugs, once the patient starts taking Luvox.

Antabuse (brand) ~ Disulfiram (generic)

Major Side Effects: Drowsiness, tired feeling, headache, restlessness, nerve pain, blurred or impaired vision, metallic or garlic taste** and sometimes dermatitis.

Interactions With Other Medications: Alcohol: Most patients, with even the smallest amount of alcohol, will experience flushing, throbbing, headaches, troubled or rapid breathing, nausea, vomiting, sweating, heart palpitations, fainting, severe weakness, extreme blurred vision and confusion. Larger amounts of alcohol can lead to more serious problems, including seizures, heart attack and death. **It is imperative** that this drug not be given to anyone who has had alcohol of any form 12 hours prior to taking disulfiram. This includes mouthwashes, vinegars or any liquid medications (prescription or over-the-counter). Also, any cosmetics (i.e., colognes, after-shaves, lotions or sprays) in which alcohol may be absorbed through the skin, and foods containing alcohol-based sauces or marinades should be avoided. Reactions have been known to occur for as long as up to 12 weeks after the last dose of disulfiram. Disulfiram may make some benzodiazepines such as **Valium** and **Librium** increase drowsiness in some patients. Patients on tricyclic antidepressants (such as **Elavil**, **Tofranil**, etc.) or metronidazole (**Flagyl**) may become confused or have changes in behavior. This may also happen with **Isoniazid**. This drug may also affect patients taking phenytoin (**Dilantin**), ethotoin (**Peganone**), mephenytoin (**Mesantoin**), and warfarin (**Coumadin**). **Caffeine** may increase certain side effects such as headache, heart palpitations and flushing. Patients who are allergic to pesticides and rubber products containing **thiuram** may also have an allergic reaction to this drug.

* Denotes those side effects which may increase in severity with an increase in dosage. Some patients may, however, become tolerant to certain side effects such as nausea and dizziness after a few weeks of therapy.

** Denotes side effects which may go away or lessen after 2 weeks.

Important Drug Information

The following was written by Max Rickets, an investigative health reporter, and author of *the Great Anxiety Escape*.

Consumer Reports hits drugs hard: Xanax, Halcion, Prozac Cited.

Consumer Reports (CR) (1/93) issued a major indictment against Xanax (Upjohn), Halcion (Upjohn) and Prozac (El Lily) - hot-selling psychoactive drugs.

Citing data from Upjohn-funded studies used to gain the Xanax's approval as an antipanic drug, the magazine revealed a disturbing "remarkable picture." People who stayed on Xanax for the full 8 weeks of one study had no better relief from anxiety than those on placebo—in fact those on Xanax were worse off than they had been at the beginning of the study. The study "showed clearly how severe the 'rebound' effect of Xanax withdrawal is."

Many believe these pills have led to the dangerous prescription drugging of America.

There are very real dangers inherent in psychoactive drugs as evidenced by government agencies reports and the manufacturers pre-FDA approval studies.

CR noted, "Xanax is just the latest in a long line of tranquilizers that have promised to deliver psychiatry's holy grail: relief from anxiety with no significant side effects. And like the pills that came before it. Xanax has fallen short . . no pill can deliver peace without a price . . . benzodiazepines . . . have held an uneasy place in American culture for three decades . . . Xanax has now turned out to be addictive than Valium itself . . . causing rage and hostility . . . two major problems: physical dependency and sedation."

"How did such a flawed drug become a pharmacological superstar?" asks *CR,* while noting, "Xanax does not represent a remarkable treatment so much as a marketing coup . . .

Upjohn . . . proceeded to spend lavishly on studies to see whether Xanax could be used to treat panic disorder, and enlisted highly respected consultants in the effect...Well before the results were published, Upjohn used the research to promote its drug . . .But, despite the ads' claims, the study produced highly ambiguous results."

CR labeled Halcion and Prozac "high notoriety," commenting that they "have been reported to induce irrational behavior, including outbursts of murderous violence and suicide attempts . . . Lawsuits have been brought against their manufacturers, seeking damages for cases of suicide and assault committed by people taking the drugs."

Xanax, Halcion and Prozac all have histories of extensive potential for hazardous side effects including death. They are all very costly. Xanax sells for $72.55 per 100 mg. bottle. Translation: $725,500 per kilogram! Street drug dealers must very envious.

In sharp contrast to the careers of these highly toxic, dangerous and costly psychoactive drugs, one natural food constituent, which used to play a highly effective, safe and inexpensive role in the treatment of stress-disorders such as insomnia, anxiety, depression and obsessive-compulsiveness is no longer available to Americans.

L-tryptophan, a safe amino acid never implicated in a death or injury in its uncontaminated form, remains an "illegal drug" in the United States as part of the Food and Drug Administration (FDA) campaign "to protect the American public."

Why is the FDA protecting the drug industry and their hosts of dangerous pharmaceuticals while barring Americans from freedom of choice in natural nutrients and health food and pet feed stores. When such information implies therapeutic benefit, the on premises product is regarded as an illegal non FDA approved drug. On the other hand, consumers do not receive adequate written and verbal notice of potential adverse side effects of pharmaceutical products; and yet oftentimes these products have known potential for harm and death.

Even the General Accounting Office (GAO) has noted that the FDA method of preapproval evaluation and post-approval monitoring of drugs is woefully inadequate. The U.S. Senate Office of Technology Assessment (OTA) has expressed alarm at the neurotoxicity of many top-selling pharmaceutical products, particularly psychoactive drugs as the benzodiazepines, most notably Halcion and Xanax.

Freedom of Choice: The FDA, the AMA and the pharmaceutical industry have created a situation in this country where citizens of sound mind and judgment may not chose how and why they might attain and sustain health and prevent disease. Nutrients which are claimed to prevent conditions and disease are deemed by the FDA to be "drugs." Their marketing, distribution and employment are regulated as "drugs." Practitioners who do not belong to allopathic medical associations, and even those who do but choose to use natural methods of healing, are subject to fine and imprisonment. FDA opinions are considered infallible; AMA and FDA protocol are regarded as absolute science. Contrary opinions and practices are often considered illegal. Why is this? Who is profiting?

Power corrupts. Today, the FDA, the AMA and the pharmaceutical cartel all have far too much power. The erosion of freedom continues. One by one, alternatives are being driven out or underground by the abuse of financial, regulatory and political power of the medical monopoly-the American *sickness industry.*

In matters of health, many well intended and highly educated scientist, bureaucrats and political leaders, as well as much of the public at large, are victims of their own incorrect educational experiences—experiences which may be considered more of *indoctrination* than *education.*

In 1991, two times Nobel laureate Linus Pauling, Ph.D. published an article in the *Journal of Orthomolecular Medicine* detailing chronic vitamin C deficiency as being the primary cause of cardiovascular disease in humans. This article had been accepted for publication by the *Proceedings of the National Academy of Sciences* on June 11, 1991; under questionable circumstances, the editor of that publication later revoked the acceptance to publish.

Why? Why is the American public and why are American medical doctors being kept ignorant of vital information such as this? Why are there no major profit incentives for wellness in America? Why are the financial rewards on disease and not on health? Why is there such a systematic bias against natural menthols of attaining and sustaining well-being in the so called "health care" delivery system?

It is a fundamental responsibility of each of us to become well informed and to exercise our individual and collective lawful political means to rectify the abuses which confront us today. Among the organizations which are in the forefront in the fight to regain our health care liberties, and which are well worth joining today are National Council for Improved Health, Citizens for Health, and Nutritional Health Alliance.

References

Adams, Ruth and Frank Murray. *Megavitamin Therapy.* New York: Larchmont Books, 1980.

Adour, K., R. Hilsinger, and F. Byl. *American Otolaryngology Annual Meeting Review Notes.* Dallas, Texas. October 7- 11, 1985.

Barbeau, A. *Archives Neurology.* Vol. 30 (1982), pp. 52-58.

Beckmann, H., D. Athen, M. Oheanu, and R. Zimmer. "DL-phenylalanine Versus Imipramine: A Double Blind Controlled Study." *Archives Psychiatric Nervenkr.* Vol. 227 (1979).

Benowitz, Neal L. "Pharmacologic Aspects of Cigarette Smoking and Nicotine Addiction." *The New England Journal of Medicine.* Nov. 17, 1988.

Bergland, Richard. *The Fabric of the Mind.* New York: Viking Penguin, Inc., 1985, pp. 80-98.

Berman, J. R. "Progabide, A New GABA Mimetric Agent in Clinical Use." *Clinical Neuropharmacology,* 1985.

Blum, Kenneth. *Handbook of Abusable Drugs.* New York: Gardner Press, Inc., 1984, pp. 5, 205.

Blum, Kenneth and Michael C. Trachtenberg. *Some Things You Should Know About Alcoholism.* Houston, Texas: MATRIX Technologies, Inc., 1988.

Bond, Michael. *Pain, Its Nature, Analysis, and Treatment.* New York: Churchill Livingstone, 1979), p. 102.

Booker, Jack E. "Pain It's All in Your Patient's Head (Or is It?)." *Nursing 82.* March, pp. 47-51.

Borison, et al. "Metabolism of the Antidepressant Amino Acid, L-phenylalanine." *Fellows of American Society of Experimental Biology Meeting Notes.* April 9-14, 1978.

Borum, P. R. *Annual Review Nutrition.* Vol. 3 (1983), pp. 233-259.

Borum, P. R. *Nutrition Review.* Vol. 39 (1981), pp. 285-390.

Braverman, Eric R. and Carl C. Pfeiffer. *The Healing Nutrients Within: Facts, Findings and the New Research on Amino Acids.* New Canaan, Connecticut: Keats Publishing Co., Inc., 1987, pp. 8, 12-13, 24, 29-58, 120-127, 306-314, 330-331.

Breggin, Peter R., M.D. *Toxic Psychiatry.* New York: St. Martin's Press, 1994.

Breggin, Peter R., M.D. *Talking Back to Prozac.* NewYork: St. Martin's Press, 1994.

Brenton, Myron and eds. *Emotional Health.* Emmaus, PA: Rodale Press, 1985, p. 129.

Bresler, David E. with Richard Trubo. *Free Yourself From Pain.* New York: Simon and Schuster, 1979, p. 298.

Chaitow, Leon. *Amino Acids in Therapy.* Rochester, Vermont: Thorsons Publishers, Inc., 1985.

Cherchi, A. et al. *American Journal of Cardiology.* Vol. 33 (1979), pp. 300-306.

Colombetti, G. and S. Monti. *European Physiology Congress Proceedings.* 1st Quarter, No. 2. 1971, pp. 45-53.

Devlin, T. M. *Textbook of Biochemistry.* New York: Wiley Press, 1982.

Diamond, Seymour and Jose Medina. "Headaches." *Clinical Symposia.* Vol. 33, No. 2 (1981).

Dietrich, Schneider-Helmert. "Interval Therapy with L-tryptophan in Severe Chronic Insomniacs," *International Pharmacopsychiatry.* Vol. 16 (1981), pp. 162-173.

Essman, W. B., ed. *Nutrients and Brain Function.* Switzerland: Karger, 1987, pp. 2-3, 164.

Feldberg and Hetzel. *Food Technology.* Vol. 12 (1958).

Fischer, E., H. Spatz, J. M. Saaverdra, H. Reggiani, A. H. Miro, and B. Heller. "Urinary Elimination of Phenylethylamine." *Biological Psychiatry.* Vol. 2, No. 2 (1972).

Fox, Arnold and Barry Fox. *DLPA, To End Chronic Pain and Depression.* New York: Pocket Books, 1985, pp. 147-199.

Fruton, Joseph and Sofia Simmonds. *General Biochemistry.* New York: Wiley, 1958, p. 792.

Gaby, Alan. *B-6, The Healing Nutrient.* New Canaan, Connecticut: Keats Publishing, Inc., 1984, pp. 58-62.

Garrett, R. C. and U. G. Waldmeyer. *The Pill Book of Anxiety and Depression.* New York: Bantam Books, 1985, p. 9.

Garrison, Robert Jr. *Lysine, Tryptophan, and Other Amino Acids.* (New Canaan, Connecticut: Keats Publishing, Co., Inc., 1982), pp. 2-9.

Garzya, G. and R. M. Amico. *International Journal Tissue Reactions.* Vol. 11 (1980), pp. 175-180.

Gelenberg, Alan J. et al. "Tyrosine for the Treatment of Depression." *American Journal of Psychiatry.* (May 1980), pp. 622-623.

Gerald, Michael C., *Pharmacology, An Introduction to Drugs.* (New York: Prentice-Hall, 1981), pp. 30-31.

Gerber, Harris, and Frizzel. "Treatment of Rheumatoid Arthritis with Histidine - A Double Blind Trial." *Arthritis and Rheumatism.* (Jan.-Feb. 1973).

Gerner, H., D. A. Gorelick, D. H. Catlin, and C. H. Li. "Behavioral Effects of Beta-endorphin in Depression and Schizophrenia." *Endorphins and Opiate Antagonists in Psychiatric Research, Clinical Implications.* New York: Plenum Press, 1982.

Goldberg, I. "Tyrosine in Depression." *Lancet.* (August 1980):

Goodheart, Robert S. and Maurice E. Shils. *Modern Nutrition in Health and Disease.* Philadelphia: Lea & Febiger, 1980, pp. 1220-1221.

Grant, Larry A. "Amino Acids in Action." *Let's Live.* (August, 1983), p. 63.

Greenstein, J. F. and M. Winitz. *Chemistry of the Amino Acids.* New York: Wiley Press, 1961.

Growden, A., Wurtman and Wurtman, eds. "Neurotransmitter Precursors in the Diet." *Nutrition and the Brain.* New York: Raven Press, 1979, pp. 117-181.

Harper, Harold A. *Review of Physiological Chemistry.* Los Altos, California: Lange Medical Publications, 1969, p. 29.

Heller, B. "Pharmacological and Clinical Effects of D-phenylalanine in Depression and Parkinson's Disease." *Modern Pharmacology-Toxicology.* 1985.

Kagan, C., R. Griffith, and A. Norins. *Dermatologica.* Vol. 156. (1978).

Khaleeluddin, K. and W. Philpott. "Data Sheet." Philpott Medical Center, Oklahoma City, Oklahoma, 1980.

King, Robert B. "Pain and Tryptophan," *Journal Neurosurgery.* Vol. 53 (July, 1980), pp. 48-50.

Lader, Malcolm. *Introduction to Psychopharmacology.* Kalamazoo, Michigan: The Upjohn Co., 1983.

Lader, Malcolm. *Introductions to Psychopharmacology.* Kalamazoo, MI: The Upjohn Co., 1983, pp. 99-100.

Leibovitz, Brian. *Carnitine, The Vitamin B_T Phenomenon.* New York: Dell Books, 1984, pp. 1318-1329.

Meister, A. *Biochemistry of the Amino Acids.* New York: Academic Press, 1975.

Milam, James R. and Katherine Kethcam. *Under the Influence.* (New York: Bantam Books, 1983), pp. 31-37, 38.

Mills, Kirk C., M.D. "Serotonin Syndrome." *American Family Pyhsician.* October 1995. p. 1475.

New Frontiers in Pain Control: Alternatives to Drugs and Surgery (Pacific Palisades, CA: Center for Intergral Medicine, 1978), p. 20.

Newbold, H. L. *Mega-Nutrients for Your Nerves.* New York: Peter Wyden Publishing, 1975.

Norden, Michael J. *Beyond Prozac. New* York, New York: HarperCollins Publisher, Inc., 1995

Pauling, Linus. *Orthomolecular Psychiatry.* San Francisco: Freeman and Co., 1973.

Pearson, D., and R. Shaffer. *Nutritional Consultants.* (November-December, 1980), p. 12.

Pearson, Durk and Sandy Shaw. *Alcohol.* Huntington Beach, California: International Institute of Natural Health Sciences, Inc., 1981, p. 20.

Pfeiffer, Carl C. *Mental and Elemental Nutrients.* New Canaan, Connecticut: Keats Publishing Co., Inc., 1975, pp. 382-383.

Phelps, Janice and Alan E. Nourse. *The Hidden Addiction and How to Get Free.* Boston: Little, Brown and Co., 1986, pp. 35-41, 79-85.

Pickens, Roy W. and Leonard L. Heston, eds. *Psychiatric Factors in Drug Abuse.* New York: Grune & Stratton, 1979, pp. 1-238.

Pickup, Dixon, Lowe, and Wright. "Serum Histidine in Rheumatoid Arthritis: Changes Induced by Antirheumatic Drug Therapy." *The Journal of Rheumatology.* Vol. 17, No. 1 (1980).

Psychopharmacology Update. Providence, RI: Manisses Communications Group, Inc., 1996.

Rapp, Doris J. *Allergies and Your Family.* Buffalo: Practical Allergy Research Foundation, 2nd edition, 1990.

Ricketts, Max, with Edward Bien. *The Great Anxiety Escape Guidebook.* In preparation.

Roe, Daphne A. *Drug-Induced Nutritional Deficiencies.* Westport, Connecticut: Avi Publishing Co., 1978, pp. 200-201, 204- 208.

Rose, W. C., D. E. Leach, J. J. Coon, and G. F. Lamberg. "The Amino Acid Requirements of Man. The Phenylalanine Requirement." *The Journal of Biological Chemistry.* Vol. 213 (1955).

Sabelli, H. and A. D. Mosnaim. "Phenylethlamine Hypothesis of Affective Behavior." *American Journal of Psychiatry.* Vol. 131 (1974).

Sahley, Billie J. *The Anxiety Epidemic.* San Antonio, Texas: The Watercress Press, 1986, pp. 7, 19-27, 39-48.

Saifer, Phyllis and Merla Zellerbach. *Detox.* New York: Ballantine Books, 1984, pp. 100, 101-105, 113, 135, 136-137.

Schatzberg, Alan F., M.D. and Charles B. Nemeroff, M.D., Ph.D. *The American Psychiatric Press Textbook of Psychopharmacology.* Washington, D.C.: American Psychiatric Press, Inc., 1995.

Shader, Richard I., ed. *Manual of Psychiatric Therapeutics.* Boston: Little, Brown, and Co., 1984, pp. 213, 273, 289.

Shader, Richard I., *Brain.* New York: Raven Press, 1979.

Shive, W., et al. "Glutamine in Treatment of Peptic Ulcer," *Texas State Journal of Medicine.* Vol. 53 (1957).

Slagle, Priscilla. *The Way Up From Down.* New York: St. Martin's Press, 1987, pp. 113, 142-145, 149, 241-247.

Smith, Bernard H. and Antonio Rosich-Pla. "The Biochemistry of Mental Illness." *Psychosomatics.* (April, 1979), p. 282.

Smith, Lendon. *Feed Yourself Right.* New York: Dell Publishing Co., Inc., 1983, pp. 33, 108, 112.

Spatz, H., B. Heller, M. Nachon, and E. Fischer. "Effects of D-phenylalanine on Clinical Picture and Phenylethylaminuria in Depression." *Biological Psychiatry.* Vol. 10, No. 2 (1975).

Stein, et al. "Memory Enhancement by Central Administration of Norepinephrine." *Brain Research.* Vol. 84 (1975), pp. 329-335.

Trickett, Shirley. *Coming Off Tranquilizers.* New York: Thorson Publishing Group, 1986, pp. 29, 30-39, 100.

White, A., et al. *Principles of Biochemistry.* New York: McGraw-Hill, 1978, pp. 1120, 1241-1264.

Wolfe, Sidney M., M.D. and Rose-Ellen Hope, R.Ph. *Worst Pills Best Pills II.* Washington, DC: Public Citizen Health Research Group. 1993.

TO ORDER
CALL 1-800-669-CALM

Name _____

Address _____

City _____ State _____ Zip _____

BOOKS

The Anxiety Epidemic (Dr. Billie J. Sahley)	$9.95
Is Ritalin Necessary? book (Dr. Billie J. Sahley)	$5.00
Malic Acid and Magnesium for Fibromyalgia and Chronic Pain (Dr. Billie J. Sahley)	$3.95
Control Hyperactivity A.D.D. Naturally book (Dr. Billie J. Sahley)	$8.95
Chronic Emotional Fatigue (Dr. Billie J. Sahley)	$3.95
The Melatonin Report (Dr. Billie J. Sahley)	$3.95
Breaking The Sugar Addiction book (Dr. K. Birkner)	$8.95
Orthomolecular Directory of Physicians and Therapists	$10.00

AUDIO CASSETTES by Dr. Billie J. Sahley - $10 Each

Anxiety	Escape
Anxiety / Panic Attacks - Causes & Control	Fear
	Forgiving and Healing
Anger	Guilt
Being, Your Way	Letting Go
Communication	Hyperactivity - Causes & Control
Depression	Phobias

Products Catalog (No Shipping Charge) $4

SUBTOTAL _____

Texas Residents ADD 7.75% Sales Tax _____

Shipping $3 (first item $3; $1 subsequent)** _____

TOTAL** _____

Personal Checks are held for 10 working days. To expedite order, send money order.

MC / Visa/ Discover _ _ _ _ - _ _ _ _ - _ _ _ _ - _ _ _ _

Signature _____ Exp. Date ____/____

Send To: Pain & Stress Center
         5282 Medical Drive, Suite 160, San Antonio, TX 78229-6023

** Canadian & Other Foreign Countries ADD $8 to the above amounts.
We accept World Money Orders or MC / Visa / Discover ONLY!

About the Authors

Billie J. Sahley, Ph.D. is Executive Director of the Pain & Stress Center and Nutrition and Vitamin Center of San Antonio. She is a Board Certified Medical Psychotherapist-Behavior Therapist, and an Orthomolecular Therapist. She is a Diplomate in the American Academy of Pain Management. Dr. Sahley is a graduate of the University of Texas, Clayton University School of Behavioral Medicine, and U.C.L.A. School of Integral Medicine. Additionally, she has studied advanced nutritional biochemistry through Jeffrey Bland, Ph.D, Director of HealthComm. She is a member of the Huxley Foundation / Academy of Orthomolecular Medicine, Academy of Psychosomatic Medicine, North American Nutrition and Preventive Medicine Association. In addition, she holds memberships in the Sports Medicine Foundation, American Association of Hypnotherapists, and American Mental Health Counselors Association. She is also on the Scientific and Medical Advisory Board for Inter-Cal Corporation. Dr. Sahley is author of *The Anxiety Epidemic*, and *The Natural Way to Control Hyperactivity, Chronic Emotional Fatigue, Malic Acid and Magnesium For Fibromyalgia and Chronic Pain Syndrome, The Melatonin Report* and numerous audio cassette tapes. She is coauthor of *Breaking Your Addiction Habit* book. In addition, Dr. Sahley has 2 U.S. patents for SAF and Calms Kids (SAF For Kids).

Kathy Birkner is a Pain Therapist at the Pain & Stress Center in San Antonio. She is a Registered Nurse, Certified Registered Nurse Anesthetist, Registered Massage Therapist, and Orthomolecular Therapist. She is a Diplomate in the American Academy of Pain Management. She attended Brackenridge Hospital School of Nursing, University of Texas at Austin, Southwest Missouri State University, and Clayton University. She holds degrees in nursing, nutrition, and behavior therapy. Dr. Birkner has done graduate studies through the Center for Integral Medicine and U.C.L.A. Medical School under the direction of Dr. David Bresler. Additionally, she has studied advanced nutritional biochemistry through Jeffrey Bland, Ph.D, Director of HealthComm. She is a member of American Association of Nurse Anesthetists, Texas Association of Nurse Anesthetists, American Association of Pain Management, American College of Osteopathic Pain Management and Sclerotherapy and American Association of Counseling and Development. She is author of *Breaking Your Sugar Habit Cookbook* and coauthor with Dr. Sahley of the audio cassette tape, *Therapeutic Uses of Amino Acids* and *Breaking Your Addiction Habit* book.